Stepping Towards Mastery

A Spiritual Course On Healing

Volume I

Dr. Jane E. Rackley

CONTENTS

PREFACE

Much has happened in my life and on this planet since the year 2014 when I published my first book, *Love Yourself and Be Healed:Awakening*. Hopefully, we each have advanced in our spiritual journey a great deal during these years. Shortly after 2017 when I published the accompanying workbook, *20 Weeks to Transformation*, I facilitated a study group of this course.

It was my conviction during this time that I thought every person should be able to complete this course during the 20-week time frame that I had outlined. I discovered very quickly that I was incorrect in my assumption.

Although our group was relatively small, we represented a variety of backgrounds, those of us actively pursuing our spiritual journey for 30 years or longer, those who had knowingly been pursuing their spiritual journey for roughly five years and the rest who were somewhere in the middle. Since most of us had participated in many other types of spiritual study groups, and were active members of a Unity Church, I had the incorrect assumption that all of us could easily move through this course during a 20-week time frame.

Since I had facilitated many other book studies on a variety of spiritual topics and courses including *A Course on Miracles,* during at least a 10-year time, I thought I had this structured very well. Silly Me!

It was my discovery within a few short weeks of starting my course, that each of us in the study group were at different levels and needed to advance at a different rate. I know that I had to stretch myself quite a bit to keep up with the pace even as the facilitator, and very quickly nearly everyone except one other person in our group was unable to keep up at the regular pace. Each of the other individuals were consistently behind a chapter or so, and even a couple of people shortly after we began started to flounder a bit and admitted they felt a little lost. I soon discovered the concepts which I *thought* were covered adequately on certain basic spiritual fundamentals in my book apparently were not covered well enough at all.

So nearly ten years later, hopefully I'm a little wiser and I have revised this book and formatted it in a completely different way. Some of the material is the same as the previous book, however, there are places where there is new material that has been added to ensure that certain topics can be understood by all. I have cut certain things out of the workbook which I discovered do not seem essential. Also, I incorporated the exercises from the workbook directly, so it becomes an all-in-one book. Finally, I have segmented this book into shorter chapters and multiple volumes. It is my hope that this will ensure that these books are easier to study and make progress. I have been given directions specifically on this topic from the group who have been advising me from the higher dimensions on my other projects. At this moment I have no idea how many volumes in total there will be in this course. It seems as if I nearly complete one book, then the wellspring breaks through with more topics.

Know that I simply facilitate the information which flows through me from a higher place into these books. Although there certainly is a portion which comes from my own personal spiritual journey and experiences, the rest is from divine sources, and I am simply a messenger.

Since this course seems to be an undetermined number of volumes, it was my decision to give this a different name than my previous book. The new title seems to be a more appropriate title to describe the type of work one might expect from this series of books.

Each of us every day is climbing step-by-step to a higher level of awareness and consciousness. As we climb, we see the next step that we need to take and leave the steps that we took previously behind. Those steps left behind are needed for those who are moving on their journey as well.

It has been explained to me that this work and my future works that I am currently writing are considered *valid* and are important during this time on our earth. I needed to look up what *valid* means to us. The two best definitions that seem to fit are: 1. sound, just, or well-founded. And 2. having force, weight, or cogency; authoritative.

As I stated before, I am simply the facilitator as I write these books. The ideas that come through have been given to me as, I stated previously, either through personal experiences and/or inspirations and ideas which have been gifted to me from divine sources.

It is my hope that if you find that you resonate with this work, then you may use this to take those next steps higher on your own personal spiritual journey. This book is designed so that each chapter with the exercises should take about 20 to 30 minutes to complete. I also highly recommend it to be a self-study course. I do not recommend using this in a book study. Each individual can progress through this at her/his own natural pace, as this will give the greatest benefit.

Another thing which has been suggested to me is that it is important to re-study certain spiritual books periodically. These books are the type which are excellent to complete studying, then to restudy it again a couple of years later. You will likely pick up new information that either you did not notice previously, or information that might assist you in an unexpected way. This practice also will help you to better absorb the spiritual principles and practices to strengthen your spiritual foundation. I know that every time I have picked up a book that I previously read maybe a few years earlier, I was amazed that I found several new pearls of wisdom that perfectly assisted me during that time.

What Is *That Something* That's Missing?

Starting at about the age of four, a child begins to tell others she can't wait until she gets to go to kindergarten and can be with all the other kids her age. She is excited that she will finally be like the older kids, and even get to ride on the school bus. She arrives in kindergarten and is happy for the first month or two. Then she overhears at recess one of the first graders crooning, "You are a bunch of babies because you still take '*little naps*' and we don't." So now she can't wait to *really* be like the big kids and not have to take a nap in school. She finally gets to first grade, and soon discovers that the second graders are allowed to go on field trips to places like the zoo. She tells her parents that *now* she can hardly wait to be in second grade.

She makes it into second grade and is happy to finally go on to her first field trip. Then her best friend tells her that she can't wait until they get to fourth grade, 'cause her older brother just got a *real* locker and gets to change classes and has *several* different teachers instead of just one. She agreed that would really be great, and it would be a lot of fun to decorate their lockers. She felt like 4th grade took forever to arrive. She thought it was cool to change classes and to put a poster of the latest cute boyband up in her locker. Shortly thereafter, she finds out that the sixth graders get to have a spring dance. She and her friends giggled at the prospect of dancing with the boys, and started thinking about how much longer they would have to wait.

Two years later, the dance came and went, and next they wanted to hurry up and get to junior high because then they could finally be out of grade school and be away from the 'little kids'. Junior high came, and she couldn't wait to get to high school for the same reasons. Once she was in high school, she couldn't wait to drive a car and finally graduate so *then* she could *really* start her life and go to college. Once in college, she thought she would have freedom to get away from her parents. She arrived in college and found that freedom but discovered that it was a lot of hard work still being in school. She decided she would be happy once she graduated and *then* she could *really* get her life going. She graduated from college and found her first job.

She looked at her life after a few months in her new job and felt like *something* was still missing. She finally contemplated that if she could buy a nicer car than the one she had been driving since her senior year in high school, and a house and maybe get married to her boyfriend, *that* would be the answer. Two years later she managed all three, but really felt like there still must be *something else*. A couple of her friends already had their first baby, maybe that was it, time to have children. She had two, and she found that she was absolutely correct that having children seemed to help her forget most of the time whatever it was that seemed missing. She was busier than ever and no longer had the time or energy to analyze any of that for a while. One year turned into two, and eventually several, and both of her kids were in school. Finally, two months before the youngest child graduates from high school, she shudders to wonder what's next? She notices *that feeling* starting to creep in again, just like the one she remembered nearly two decades ago. It seemed to be slowly slipping back up to the surface. She wonders... maybe after graduation, then *I* should go back to school? Maybe that's it. I just need to go back to school and change my career. On and on it goes, throughout all the rest of her life.

During the last days of her lifetime, she finally has the time to reflect upon the past evaluating whether she truly accomplished everything. Once again, that feeling is there, only this time not nearly as subtle as it had been in the years before. As she realizes that her life is now *nearly* at the end, she feels more unsettled as her thoughts continue to search for the answers. Did I accomplish everything? Was there more? Did I miss something here? What was it? Her mind grapples with these attempting to capture the elusive answers. She wondered why she had never anticipated all those years earlier that these things were so important. Finally, all at once it comes to her. She takes a long and drawn breath, as if finally remembering a long-lost secret. A tear begins to swell up and then spills down the corner of her eye.

She awakens the following morning hearing soft whispers and exchanges the last glimpses of her husband and children gathered at her bedside. A few moments later, she gently drifts away...

How many people would say, "That sounds like a pretty good life to me. Isn't that how we are *supposed* to live?" This is the mainstream way of thinking life should progress, but is this *really* why we are here? What is the purpose of life? Should we pause to ask this, or simply keep on moving in all our busyness and belief that we simply are *going with the flow*?

I remember distinctly when I was age eight sitting in my room, and praying in the hardest and most focused way my eight-year young being could muster.

"God, please tell me the meaning of life. What's the purpose of life?" I paused quietly, hoping I might somehow receive an instant answer. I kept my eyes closed tightly, still listening with all my might. I didn't hear the direct reply I expected. So, I finally relented my effort for the night and went to sleep.

The following day I thought, the answer must be here somewhere. Maybe I need to go look for it. So, the next time my babysitter took my brother and I to the public library I went into the philosophy aisle. I dragged several huge books off the shelves, and carefully searched through them to select the books that had my answer. Since I could only check out up to six books at a time, I was meticulous and chose only the best ones. During our walk back home, the books were nearly too heavy for me to carry. Halfway back, my babysitter helped by carrying one of the larger ones for me.

As soon as we were home, I took the books straight to my room, and excitedly started flicking through the pages. Some of them were written by, and about, historical people who lived hundreds of years ago having names like Aristotle, Plato, and Socrates. A couple of the titles described *The History of Modern Philosophy* as well as *The Compendium of Early Philosophy*. I finally grabbed one of the books and decided to start at the beginning.

Years ago, my mother divulged to me that when I took my first Iowa basic skills test in the fifth grade, my reading level was evaluated equivalent to that of an 11th grader. That helped me to better understand why I always got into trouble with my teachers for reading ahead in the book during reading class. However, this occurred in the summer after I had only completed the third grade. So even though I was apparently an avid and advanced reader at an early age, at best my reading ability and comprehension at this time might have been at a fourth or fifth grade level.

I began to read the first page. I stopped at about every third or fourth word which was long and might as well had been in a foreign language. I couldn't comprehend anything. I threw aside that book and swiped up another. I flipped to the beginning. This time I attempted to read the first paragraph, second, and third to see if I could somehow get it to make sense. I then rummaged to the middle of the book and tried again, thinking a different part of the book might be easier. I repeated the process in each different book thinking that I must be able to understand *at least* one of them. I was sure that the answer I needed was somehow contained in those books. I finally gave up for that day, and then tried again at least a couple of more times later.

The following week I schlepped those books back, and as I thumped them onto the counter the librarian peered over her half glasses giving me an amused smile. I am sure she was tickled at me. I figured if my answer was in any of those books, I might have to wait a few more years to find out.

I was fortunate to ask this question at an early age. Even though I didn't obtain the instantaneous answer I thought, this definitively started me on my path. The answers started to come. They came in a way that I could understand at the age of eight, then again at the age of nine, at ten, eleven, at thirty, at forty and every other day of my life. I learned that when we ask, we are given what we can understand from our own viewpoint. If I had been given every answer to my questions at the age of eight, then there would be nothing left to discover in my journey. Where is the fun and adventure of that? All the perfect situations, people, relationships, and spiritual teachers each show up at precisely at the right time and place.

What is unfortunate is that so many people meander through life and never ask these important questions. Instead of recognizing there is more, and grasping for it, countless people simply move through the daily motions blindly. The journey can be much longer and arduous when we are caught in the blinding web of the outer world. Hopefully, there comes an event or time which shakes our routine, and causes us to first question, and then to seek out this other *something.*

Congratulate yourself if you are reading this book at *any time* during your life. This means you must have asked yourself some of the big questions in life. Most people at some point ask themselves these, but often they are pushed to the back burner. Often, we think yes, I'd like to someday take the time to look into that, but right now I'm too busy with.... (fill in anything).

What's the meaning of life? Why are we here? What's our purpose here? Where did we come from before coming here? Where will we go after we leave here? What's *really* the point of our living here from day to day? Why do some people live longer than others? Why are some people's lives easier(harder) than others? Is there *really* a God out there who decides and runs everything here? Why do things happen in the world (our lives) the way they happen? Are we *truly* the only inhabited planet in the universe? These are the kind of inquiries that a four-year-old will often ask adults, but within only a few years later will become distracted and no longer ask.

Recently I attended a meditation group. After finishing up the evening, people were slowly coming back to the outer world and giving each other the routine good-bye hugs. One woman who had started attending within the last few months blurted out," I just have to say, that I am just *so* grateful that I have found this...this church, community, just everything!" She choked back the emotion in her throat," I can't get over that I have been just sitting with my beliefs doing *nothing* and staying in the same place for years! For years!" she cried out," Now, for the first time in *years* I feel like I am *really* growing again!" She choked back a couple of tears as a grand wave of gratitude washed completely over her.

It is so rewarding to witness someone who is overcome with joy in the realization that they are back on their journey of awakening. That time in a person's life, when they have finally realized that there is *something* we might be here to find in our life, which has nothing to do with the typical day-to-day outer world activities. This is the time I am sure there are unseen ones rejoicing in other realms, as one more being on this planet has finally started the process of *awakening.*

That one elusive *something* which countless people grasp often in all the wrong places throughout their whole life, is simply to *awaken.* Yet there are still many who may state, "Why do I need to *awaken* and what purpose would that serve?" There are quite a few who might argue, "But I am happy, I have a good job and a great family. I even grew up in a church where I learned everything that I need to know. I have good values, and I follow all the rules. *Sometimes* I still attend church and think of my beliefs at times. I think this *should* be plenty!"

The problem with this way of thinking is this is all we have ever been taught that we should strive for in this life. Many people have been led to believe that there is a stopping point in life. Where it is okay to reach, and then once attaining that seemingly safe *"comfort zone,"* that is our arriving place. This is the place in which many feel they have accomplished everything they were told was important in life and can pretty much coast from there forward. This seeming "comfort zone," is really the place where most all the possible spiritual growth and journey has come to a rest or may even completely stop.

It is important that we stop and really look at our life and examine it closely at a window of about the previous five years. We need to ask ourselves questions such as: What kind of growth has occurred for me during this time? What are some of the events which have caused me to grow, and in what way? Can I name at least two or three important life lessons I have learned, and how has it caused me to become a better person? Am I able to notice clear signs in my life that I am experiencing spiritual growth? What are they? Have I actively pursued learning anything which has fed my soul? What kinds of transformative changes can I see in myself as a result? How have the patterns in my relationships with others changed and improved?

If we ask ourselves these questions and find that we can't really identify much that has changed during the previous five years, or if the only changes we can identify come from material things such as "bought a different house," then we need to recognize that we have come to rest in our "*comfort zone*." We may feel really content here, yet there is little or no growth occurring in ourselves.

We must realize, everything is always percolating just under the surface. Even as one settles in after acquiring the next better job, the next bigger house, or the next fancier car, we are never quite satisfied for long and are looking for *something* else. That *something* which is always there and patiently waiting. It is persistent in its wait and is timeless. It is that tiny whisper that pushes you onto the next search, to figure out if *this time* it will be different, and you'll find that which will really satisfy you.

What is that elusive *something* that will fulfill the deep yearnings of humanity? It is ever-present, always waiting, and eternal. It is for us to *awaken* to the true nature of ourselves. It is for us to re-member that which is our true essence, our own divinity. It is only when we *actively* pursue the understanding and experience of our own divinity, that we can finally move towards a sense of greater satisfaction and fulfillment in our lives. Every other outer world pursuit will always fall short and feel empty compared to our own progressive journey toward *awakening.*

My beloved Spiritual Teacher, Her Holiness Sai Maa has repeated many times to her students: *Do you choose to take the slow way, or take the fast route? I can appreciate those who wish to go slow, but I am here for you who choose to go fast.* Many times, throughout the years, I have watched her working with different students during our retreats. Often one of us might stand before her relating one of our issues in life. Sai Maa will guide us and help us to see whatever it is we need to approach differently. Occasionally, whatever direction Sai Maa has given will seem like an unexpected, or uncomfortable action to the student. Sai Maa will patiently attempt to redirect and explain some of the reasoning, and yet still there are times the student continues to resist Sai Maa's suggestion. After a certain point, if the student has built a strong wall of resistance and is unwilling to be open to any suggestions, Sai Maa will state," That's okay if you don't want to do the work now, then you may choose to do it during your next lifetime."

There are a few who may initially think this seems a little harsh, but this is the reality of it. Sai Maa has also related to us that her job as our Spiritual Teacher is to push us. One time she stroked her face into a giddy statue-like smile demonstrating," Going through life saying everything is fine, I'm fine, my family is fine, it's all fine, fine, fine. She shook her head back into a serious posture. When you are living your life in this way you are *not* growing. This is *why* I push you."

So, we can relate that one of the typical by-products of *awakening* might include being uncomfortable at times. Although this may seem like it is a requirement, it does not mean that we need to live a life filled with suffering or pain. There are those who experience much of this throughout life, and *still* do not recognize the lesson or message which is there for one to learn.

Also, there is a difference between allowing ourselves to be open to *awakening,* and pursuing the experiences which will bring us new growth, versus permitting ourselves to be buffeted hither and yonder experiencing painful or disharmonious situations. How do we know which of these are occurring in our life?

Think about how you feel from day to day, and week to week. You most likely are in your journey of *awakening,* if you can examine a certain measure of time, and most of it feels peaceful or a sense of inner harmony. There is a distinct feeling of being on purpose most of the time and almost an inner knowledge that you are moving forward. This doesn't imply that there will not be times of difficult events which will cause an upset. However, these incidents come and are hurdled relatively quickly and then one gets back on purpose again.

You are most likely stagnant and *not* very actively in the process of *awakening* if you examine a certain measure of time and a good portion of it feels discordant, or in a state of upheaval. During this time, you may more often have a feeling of being scattered and may feel frustration because deep down you have a sense that you are off purpose. More often you may feel like you are in a rut, and not sure how it happened or how to move out of it. Many people sometimes become so used to moving from one disharmonious situation to another, that they believe eventually that this is simply normal, and how life is supposed to be lived. When difficult events occur, it seems to take a long time to recover, and the same situations tend to recur over and over. If this continues long enough, a person may notice a moderate to high degree of emotional upset on and off which may show up eventually as depression.

It is also possible for us to have certain periods of our life in which for a few years we were experiencing growth, and then we become stagnant for a while. Sometimes one or more challenges may come, and we may simply get off track.

The important thing to remember is that it doesn't matter whether we are in the *awakening* process and experiencing rapid growth or are stuck for a bit working to get out of the muckedy-muck of outer world sludge. Regardless of which we are doing, there is no right or wrong way. *All* are destined regardless, eventually to fully awaken. This is *that something* everyone either presently seeks in our life, or eventually will try to find. The best part is that everyone *will* eventually arrive. We must ask ourselves, do I wish to move slowly, or quickly?

Awakening is every person's destiny here, regardless of if we are aware of it or not. It doesn't matter whether the religious teachings we learned as children agree with this concept. It doesn't matter if our family and friends think it is nonsense. None of this matters because it is our birthright. At some point, we eventually discover our true selves.

Homework

Obtain a good-sized lined notebook with at least 80 to 100 pages. Designate the *front half* of your notebook to keep during your day and near your bed at night. Begin paying attention to any dreams at night or insights which you may start to notice throughout your day. Oftentimes, these may come in a flash of instant awareness, or messages from other people. Start writing them down in your journal. Designate the *back half* of your notebook to write the answers to the questions of the exercise section at the back of each chapter.

It is important to reflect on and answer all the questions in the exercises before moving on to the next chapter. The exercises will help you to implement the concepts in the book into your life. This is a practical application which will help you to systematically use all the concepts and tools fully to transform your life. Each exercise builds on the previous and you will oftentimes need a portion of the earlier exercise information to complete the latter material. It is suggested that you complete each chapter and exercises at your own pace. This book is designed for anyone who really chooses to do the work to grow and create spiritual mastery in life. Remember that anything worth accomplishing in life may be simple but takes dedication and is not necessarily easy.

Exercise

At the top of your notebook on each of two to three lines write Career, Family, Spiritual, Spouse/ Partner, Friends, Health, and Education. Then list up to two major events /actions which have occurred during the last five years of each of these areas of your life. Choose major events which you feel has caused you to grow. Examples: Career: applied for a new position and was passed over. Family: had a long and much needed talk with my sister and put aside old grudges. Spiritual: Found and became actively involved in a spiritual community. Partner /Spouse: Went on a spiritual retreat with my partner. Friends: Discontinued spending time with a friend who seemed to drain my energy. Health: took a fall and fractured my elbow. Education: Completed a new certification course in my career field.

Now count the total number of events/actions you listed in your notebook. If you listed *less* than four items, it might be likely that you are hanging out in your *comfort zone*. If you counted 4 to 9 items, you are likely moving forward on your spiritual journey. If you had ten or more, it is highly likely that you are on the fast track. You might even need to take a breath and slow down a bit!

In your notebook on each of three to four lines write Career, Family, Spiritual, Partner/Spouse, Friends, Health, and Education. Now look at each event/action you listed for each category previously. Explain for each event what lesson, new understanding, or how did the event/ action cause you to grow spiritually or otherwise. Examples: Career: I was able to see a couple of months later that the position was not in my best interest. It would have led me off purpose. Family: I was able to really see my sister's side of things and listen better. I learned that my own stubbornness was causing many of our problems. Spiritual: I'm sharing with a group of like-minded people. This is allowing me to grow through fellowship, meditation, groups, and book studies. Partner/Spouse: I had greater insights about my partner's needs and experienced greater growth in myself. Friends: I learned to be a little more aware in selecting my friends. I found that it is not helpful to be with others who spend time caught up in negativity. Health: I realized this was a sign that I needed to slow down in my life, and it is important to pay attention to my surroundings. Education: I finished a certification which is aligned with my higher purpose. I will be able to serve others in a greater capacity than before. Examine what you wrote in the last exercise. Were you able to connect the events/actions in your life with a lesson or spiritual growth? If you found any part of this difficult, it is okay, as you will become better as you progress through the book.

Look at the seven categories, and notice which areas did you have the greatest amount of growth in your life? List them in your notebook. Notice which areas had the least amount of growth during the last five years? Write these in your notebook as well.

Write in your notebook what you think are the reasons for the greater areas of growth in your life. Explain what you think are the reasons for the lesser areas of growth in your life.

At this moment, we are evaluating our past to determine how much we have grown. Remember there aren't any right or wrong answers. This simply helps us to begin really seeing our life. Our intention is to move into a place of true understanding. Have I been spending a lot of time hanging out in my comfort zone? Or does it seem like I am moving forward and progressing on my spiritual journey? Once we can understand better, we can then eventually set the sail on our boat and move in the direction we choose.

What Is Truth?

Yippee! So, you figured out that we each have the same highest purpose. We are on this journey called *awakening*. Now what? There is so much information swirling around both on the information highway and everywhere else in our environment. How do we wade through everything and really make some sort of sense of it all? Does it make any sense that it would be helpful to have some sort of guideline to understand the world around us?

Sai Maa explained once how to determine if a concept is founded in truth or not. That which is truth is always *changeless*. That which is a be*lief* always *changes*. Also, look at what is in the center of the word *be**lie**f*. So that which is rooted in truth is so today, was the same 5000 years ago and still will be the same in 10,000 years from now. We can also take this teaching to the next step to recognize that truth is also *timeless*. A be*lief*, on the other hand, might be one thing today, different from 200 years ago and will change again 500 years from now.

One example of an old be*lief* system in science is that it was thought prior to the 1900's that all the continents on the planet were static and never moved. However, during the early 1900's geologists first theorized that maybe the continents drifted somewhat. Later it was determined that the theory was correct, and this drifting occurred over subterranean *plates.* Today the scientists call this phenomenon *plate tectonics.* This is the best explanation geologists understand right now. But it is possible that in another 50 more years with greater and more sensitive technology, scientists may understand there is *something else* which affects and causes the drifting and may rename it yet again differently. So, this demonstrates a concept, or be*lief* which clearly has changed over time. Although this exemplifies a scientific be*lief*, we can find numerous examples based on philosophy, religion, spirituality, health and more.

It is not as simple to choose an example of something which the vast majority of people would agree is the truth and is completely changeless. This is where *only* firsthand experience can allow one to recognize that which is *changeless* and *timeless.* If I stated that it is a truth that the essence, or soul of each person is eternal, having no beginning and no ending, there are some who would agree and then those who would disagree. So, the *only* way to *really* know that which is true, is to have encountered it directly. If we simply accept another person or group's opinion as our own, this falls back into the category of be*lief.* Everything which is established in truth, can be experienced by us directly. It is only through our *own* personal experience that we can discern what is a truth. Once we have direct knowledge, it will never leave us.

So, to be able to recognize in our life the difference between something which is a *belief* vs. *truth*, we must take that which we are evaluating through a cascade of questions.

Is the idea/concept *changeless*? This means that it always stays the same, and never changes. If the answer is yes, continue to the next question. If the answer is no, then it is a *belief.*

Is the idea/concept *timeless*? This means that it always has been the same 3000 years ago as it is today. It also means that it will still be the same in 3000 years from today. If the answer is yes, continue to the next question. If the answer is no, then it is a belief.

Is it possible for a person to *experience* first-hand the idea/concept? If the answer is yes, continue to the next question. If the answer is no, then it is a belief.

Is there any situation or outside influence which could alter the idea/concept? If the answer is yes, then it is a belief. If the answer is no, then it is a truth.

Would it be valuable to simply ask three or four questions about anything and determine if it falls into the category of a belief or truth? Would it be easier to understand everything in the world around us? Let's take the idea or concept that the continents sit on plates which are movable allowing the land of our planet to move. It is currently named *plate tectonics.* Look at question one, is it changeless? This means that it always stays the same. No, because scientists have changed this theory thinking land did not move over to modern thought that it does move. The second question, is it timeless? This means the concept was the same 3000 years ago. The answer is no. Therefore, this concept is a belief. Many concepts will rarely get past the first two questions. It doesn't take a genius to figure out that we are surrounded in a sea of many beliefs. The important thing is to be able to recognize concepts which might take a person down a rabbit hole and completely off track.

Concepts which the first two questions are a yes, can be experienced directly by a person, and cannot be altered by any outside influence always will be a truth. Some might say that these questions are useful to determine truth with a capital T.

Why is it so important for us to seek direct experiences in our life? First-hand experience is the most valuable and leads us beyond mere theoretical ideas to our own knowledge.

It might be like the first time a small child sees an airplane flying in the sky. She is told that people can fly in a plane from one place to another within a couple of hours, much faster than what it normally takes in a full day to drive. She is filled with awe and asks what it is like to fly. Her parents may attempt to describe what it is like to board the plane and take off, what the clouds look like and all that can be seen from above, and what it is like to land. She listens to all that she has been told by others who have flown in planes and tries to imagine the feeling. Years later, she finally gets to ride in a plane and finds her experience to seem completely different from all that she has been told before. She finds that it is even better than she ever had expected. Until she had her own *individual experience,* no amount of description by another person could ever have helped her to *really* know. If anyone ever asks her if she knows about flying, she will always sound a resilient *yes,* and will be able to speak to others from her own experience.

Exercise

Select three different concepts/ideas from science, spirituality, religion, health, or philosophy. Write each one into your notebook. Take each one step by step through the cascade of four questions out of this chapter and determine whether it is a belief or truth. Example: Concept: The essence or soul of each person is eternal, having no beginning or ending. Is it changeless? Yes. Is it timeless?

Yes. Can it be experienced? Yes. Can it be influenced? No. Is it a belief or truth? Truth.

Describe how being able to distinguish the difference between a belief and truth might be valuable in evaluating ideas/concepts about your health, spirituality, religion, philosophy, and science.

Pick one of your beliefs that you listed above, and state whether you feel that most people in society tend to embrace this concept/idea? Do you feel this belief is overall beneficial for the people in our society, or do you feel it is detrimental, and explain in your notebook in what way? Do you envision that this belief will eventually change in our society, and if so, what do you think it will take to cause it to shift? Explain in your notebook.

Homework

Begin paying attention to things, or insights that you may notice throughout your day. Oftentimes these may come in a flash of instant awareness, or even messages from other people. Write these down in the first half of your notebook designated as your journal.

What Is *Awakening*?

This is what it takes to be on the path of *Awakening*. It is having the thirst to actively pursue that which is *changeless* and *timeless*. It is having the desire like a child ready to take his first airplane flight to fully experience and know the truth.

Our journey of *Awakening* has many similarities to taking a flight on an airplane. We may choose to book a plane on any one or more combinations of flights which can go to countless destinations. Some flights may be long, some short. Some flights may have one or more connecting flights or be very short and direct. Each flight we take has a unique group of other people all riding with us. Some we may find are going to the same planned destination as us, and others may exit the plane at an earlier destination to go elsewhere. If we pay attention to the others on board with us, we may also notice that there are those whom we have a lot in common, and others that seem very different from us. Finally, if we look around us and notice the experience the others are having compared to ours, we will see that everyone is undergoing a completely unique event based upon his own perspective.

One man may sit completely engrossed in utilizing all his time on the flight to perform work on his electronic computer. He ignores all the activity surrounding him and speaks only to his flight attendant to specify his drink. A woman may be very uncomfortable after eating food earlier which has upset her intestinal tract. She has kept most of her focus upon going to and from the bathroom and shifting in her seat to become more comfortable. Another man is sitting deliberately distracting himself by wearing earphones playing music and keeping his eyes tightly closed. He knows he is afraid of flying, and feels if he can divert his attention away from seeing out of the window and pretend he isn't really on an airplane, he can maybe get through it. Two rows away from him there is a woman who has announced to everyone near her that her son bought her plane ticket to come see him for her 60th birthday, and this is her first time getting to fly. Someone switched seats with her so she could sit right next to the window. She spent the whole flight gasping and marveling at what it was like to see the cities from above. She excitedly watched the buildings, lakes, and even cars driving down the roads. As the aircraft coasted into its first set of clouds, her smile widened like the delight of a child being told she could play in the middle of a mud puddle. Later into the flight as the clouds became instead of white and fluffy, much darker, and dense the plane was jostled roughly about. She exclaimed, "What is this?!" A couple of people explained to her it is what is called *turbulence.* She continued, "Wow! Isn't this a lot of fun, like a rollercoaster!" Although a couple of people near her chuckled at her giddiness, the man two rows away closed his eyes tighter and turned his music up louder to keep his thoughts away from the thrashing of the plane. The man busy with his work let out a disgruntled sigh, as he was having trouble continuing to type on his keyboard with the jostling of the plane. The woman at the back of the plane was told she needed to take her seat for a bit until the turbulence stopped. She sat hoping she could keep her nausea at bay by stuffing a couple of pretzels into her mouth.

Finally, the aircraft lands and each passenger slowly file up the aisle to get off the plane. The flight attendant smiles at each passenger, thanking each of them for choosing to fly with their airline. Each person exits, and although this flight started at the same place and arrived at the same eventual destination for everyone, there are no two people who will describe their experience to another the same. Everyone rode in the same plane, had the same staff assisting, the same food choices, the same scenery, and same length of flight. However, each person later will most likely be asked," How did you like your flight?" Even if 85 people boarded the plane and exited at the same time, there would be 85 completely different answers. Each one of them would relate a completely unique experience, although most all the circumstances were nearly identical.

The man preoccupied in his work may relate, that it was a great flight as he accomplished a lot of his work up until the turbulence. Then he just wanted to hurry up and arrive, so he could get busy and be productive again. The woman who spent much of her time in and out of the bathroom, relates to others it was a lousy flight as she was sick the whole time. Her perception was the attendants didn't seem to care much about her, and even made her go back to her seat. The man who was afraid throughout the flight simply was relieved to be on solid ground. If anyone asked him about it, he would avoid answering, and simply say it was fine. The woman who savored her first flight will meet her son and speak nonstop for the first hour. She will likely relate to him every detail she can remember gleefully and thank him for such a wonderful trip.

This is precisely the way we each spend our life journey. We might be experiencing nearly identical circumstances as another, yet our focus, perception, and response to all that is occurring to us are completely different. These people each exemplify a few of the major ways we may decide to travel through our life. One may be self-absorbed and driven to live mostly through working. Ignoring most everything surrounding oneself and focusing mostly on career advancement and success is one pattern many may find themselves. Another group of people may spend much of the time during life in a state of fear or worry. They focus so much upon the possibility that something bad may happen. Much time is caught up in this battle of constant concern over things which most likely will rarely happen. Yet another group may have health issues which seemingly come up frequently throughout their life and are often a moderate to serious distraction. Lastly, there are those progressing through life being fully in the experience much of the time. These people are the ones mostly engaged and enjoying most of their life. They tend to have a variety of interests and are more balanced and tell others they love their jobs, their family, and seem genuinely happy.

Is there one of these groups we can identify ourselves in either most of the time, or a portion of the time? If so, hopefully it is in the last group. It is when we actively pursue *Awakening*, which allows us to mostly move out of the first three groups, or other less desirable group patterns into the last group. It is here where we can ultimately experience a greater sense of peace, balance, growth, and happiness during our life.

The dictionary definition of *Awakening* is: The act of starting to understand something or feel something. The root of the word is *Awaken* which means: Rouse from sleep; cause to stop sleeping. Simply by looking at this definition we might deduce that the opposite of being in a state of *Awakening* would be instead a state of *sleeping*. How many people go throughout a whole lifetime completely asleep? Unfortunately, quite a few more than we would like to see.

Another way to describe this also is the level, or degree of *awareness* we have in our life. This defined is: the knowledge or perception of a situation or fact. So, as we have already established, there are people going through life at all different levels of *awareness,* which is directly related to the degree to which a person is *awake.* We might ask in many ways how to fully understand this concept. Once I witnessed the best explanation of this ever by Sai Maa.

When Sai Maa first came to the United States she travelled back and forth across the country. During this earlier time, smaller groups would attend her retreats. I heard she was going to be in Indianapolis just for a two-hour program on a Saturday night. So, I drove up to see her. It was held in the Ebenezer Baptist Church, and all the public were invited. She had finished leading us in a meditation, singing a chant, and began teaching. She began telling us that the *only* thing we each came here to do, is to become *fully enlightened.* That this is simply it, and there is really nothing else. Basically, in just a few short sentences, she summed up the meaning of life I had asked years ago.

A man stood up and interrupted her saying," Well, I feel like I'm *already fully enlightened* and there isn't anything else I need to do." he jeered at her and continued, "A few years ago I gave my life to Christ and was saved and now I'm born again. There isn't anything else that I *need* to do now."

Sai Maa calmly explained, what you describe is that you had a certain *spiritual experience.* This is different than being enlightened. A person may have a number of different experiences such as this throughout one's lifetime. But when

28

a person becomes *fully enlightened,* this is a *state of being.* An individual afterwards is in this *constant state* of higher awareness.

The man sat down looking a little puzzled afterwards, but I understood and felt this was a great explanation. A *state of being.* The concept is very simple, but not necessarily so easy.

We came here to re-member that which we have forgotten through the process of *Awakening,* which eventually leads us to the continuous *state of being fully enlightened.* Whew! How long does it take us to figure this out? And do we really understand?

Throughout the years I have come to realize that there is truly never any end to our *Awakening.* Even when an individual eventually moves into the realm of being *fully enlightened,* this is not where it ends. At this stage there is usually a greater level of responsibility, in fully living on purpose and helping others to accomplish the same. There is never an end point where we may rest on our laurels and state, "I finally am there, and now there is nothing more to attain."

It is an infinite journey which never stops, no matter which level one has reached. A few years ago, Sai Maa would speak about one of her personal assistants and tell others that she had reached, "baby enlightenment." She attempted to explain how there were varying levels. During this time, I was still attempting to wrap my westernized brain around its importance and how all of this *enlightenment* stuff worked.

A few years later I finally let go, deciding that maybe it was one of those concepts that it would be okay if I never fully understood. A little after this, I had a dream or vision which allowed me to finally "get" how this works in our lives. I found myself on what seemed like a platform. I knew

I was on a break from my life. I was either between lifetimes, or simply taking a rest of some sort. There were a couple of other beings with me too. I seemed to know the other two who were there, and we were joyous to see each other, as if it had been quite a bit of time since we had seen each other. As we stood on this platform and walked about, there were about 15–16 identical television-like screens each showing the activities of one person on the planet. It showed exactly at that moment what activities each one was doing, and the whole scenario of their life on the screen. Each of us excitedly went from one to another watching each person and cheering them on. We seemed to know every one of them. Just above each screen there was a large red LED type display of numbers. Each person's number screen displayed different numbers. One read 374, another 414 and each one had other varying numbers. Suddenly there was a flicker as one person's numbers moved up a few digits higher. We all raced over to his screen, and watched what he was doing in his life, whooping, and hollering so happy for him. We knew that whatever decision and action he had just taken in his life moved his number up a few points higher. This activity also indicated that his level of awareness had just increased. We marveled and watched intently for a moment to see what specific circumstances and actions he had just taken, hoping to see what we might learn from him. We then stopped at every other member's screen, and we recognized and applauded those whose numbers had advanced higher since we had last seen them. Also, we noticed those numbers which hadn't moved up at all and stopped to analyze their life scenario. We sent them loving thoughts filled with hope, that they would take the needed action in their lives to start moving higher again. Later, I noticed that there were two different people's screens that were missing from the group whom I knew had previously been in our group. I asked what happened to them? I was told that the two had moved on to a different group, and a new level. Initially, I felt like I would miss them greatly, but then a feeling of joy washed over me as I knew they moved up in their awareness and went onward to have new experiences.

I returned after this detailed vision feeling much more clarity. It impressed so much upon me and has never faded with time. I experienced how much pure love we have for each other. There was no ego at all, and we truly wanted everyone to grow and expand in awareness. There was no competition, no hurry, simply learning. We cheered and encouraged each other, wanting everyone to progress and grow. I felt a hunger there to learn, grow and expand. I saw that we seem to stay in a particular group along with several others, as we continue to learn our lessons. When we finish growing all that we can at that specific level, then we move on to the next one. So, it is here that I discovered with no uncertainty, that there is not any end place. We are infinite beings on an eternal adventure of encounters, and all our possibilities of growth are limited only by whatever we can't imagine. Everything is possible and there are a never-ending number of possibilities.

I realized that *enlightenment* is not the final destination. Although it is a higher state of awareness than *un-enlightenment,* it doesn't matter whether we are there yet or not. What matters is that we are growing, learning, and progressing in our level of awareness, and not sitting stagnant. This increase in awareness and growth only occurs when we are open and actively seeking it. It is not enough for us to read a lot of books or sit and think of a few theories or ideas now and then. It is when we put our feet to the pavement and put all we learn into practice day to day, and *only* then we will be able to recognize and know that we are growing.

It is not that we love to be alone, but that we love to soar, and when we do soar, the company grows thinner and thinner until there is none at all. ...We are not the less to aim at the summits, though the multitude does not ascend them.
—Henry David Thoreau

Fortunately, throughout the history of this planet we have had several living examples of people who were able to fully step into mastery, or *full enlightenment* as many call it. Most of them lived a public enough life to attempt to lead others by being a model for the rest to follow. The Eastern portion of our world are more familiar with Gautama Buddha, who attained his mastery after sitting in the practice of meditation many years. He finally reached his full awareness after sitting many days under the Bodhi tree. His teachings and practices have been passed throughout the years and are essentially still mostly intact today in the religions of varying types of Buddhism.

Westerners are more familiar with the life of Jesus, the man who eventually became the Christ after several years of similar study and practice. His original teachings and practices have been passed throughout the years, but unfortunately are not as well intact today in the religions of varying types of Christianity.

The major thing for us to notice are that each of these people who moved into Mastery all had much in common. Each lived their life initially in the same types of circumstances as any other person, but then at an early age had the desire to know more. Each of them had the same hunger to learn, and then practiced all which they learned vigilantly. They were dedicated and determined to fully understand and experience the truth. Neither would stop practicing, nor allow themselves to become sidetracked.

Both were able to accomplish on this planet that continuous state of being *fully awakened,* or *enlightened.* After they accomplished this for themselves, they reached out to others to teach them how to do the same in their lives.

It is unfortunate that over the centuries many of the original practices which Jesus taught to his disciples during his life have become watered down, at the least. This is why at this date there are at least 41,000 different Christian religious denominations. Each one of these has a differing be*lief* system, which is slightly to vastly different from the other. The variety of Christian dogmas run the whole spectrum, such as those who be*lie*ve Jesus taught that one might die and burn in hell if one doesn't live just right. Others be*lie*ve that a person dies and stays in the grave, and only certain ones of the "chosen few" will be resurrected someday when Jesus returns. This is one be*lief* that it seems at least a portion of the Christian denominations agree with each other in some form. Most agree that there will be a *Second Coming of Christ.* This is that Jesus will someday return to our planet, and in some shape or fashion save either some, or all the people here in some way. These limitless number of differences in Christian denominations are so great, it almost looks comedy-like if we lined them all up side-by-side to each other. But it is a serious subject, as this means that the actual *changeless* truth Jesus attempted to teach others has split off into at least 41,000 different variations. All these variations do not stand up to our method of measuring the truth. They do not meet the qualifications of truth, because they are not *timeless* and *changeless.* Even a minimally adept analytical person might see, that if his actual teachings had continued untainted throughout the years, there would be only one Christian Religion today.

There are two great errors which have been passed down through the generations that many Christians have embraced. Sai Maa mentions these usually once at nearly every event of hers. She will explain this to everyone just in case there are those still caught up in the web of these Western be*lie*fs.

She will scan the room intently pointing upwards, you *must* know there is no God *out there* sitting watching you, and waiting to do things to you if you are bad. She next moves her hand over her heart, this is it *right here*. You have *everything* here. You must *know* this.

Later, in a lighter mood, Sai Maa explains, "Don't be thinking that Jesus plans to come back to this planet. He *already* came here and there are those who think he is coming again. Why would he even *want* to come back here anyway? So the people here could kill him again? Jesus is off doing many other things now and is much too busy to come back here." Her amusement dissipates and she pauses with urgency. "*You* are the ones you have been waiting for, *you* are the second coming of Christ. It is time for *you* to wake up and re-member you are that. You are *everything*!"

Exercise

Explain and describe in your notebook the difference between *awakening* and *enlightenment*.

What do you feel is the importance of awakening? What do you feel is the importance of enlightenment?

Look back at your exercise from chapter one. Choose two events /actions you listed. Write the first event/action you selected on the left side of your notebook and the second event/action on the right side. Think about what other areas of your life such as career, family, spiritual, spouse/partner, friends, health, and education you have noticed that these actions/events have affected. Describe this in your notebook below each event. Finally, describe in what way today each of these same areas of your life seem to have shifted, or have been altered by each of these actions/events. Example: Took a fall and fractured my elbow. I realized that this was a sign that I needed to slow down in my life and pay better attention to my surroundings. This also affected my career as I had to slow down and had to get help with many of my activities at work. It influenced my family life as I was unable to perform several regular household and outdoor chores. My spiritual life was influenced because I could see that I had created the situation by being critical of others in a similar situation. Today I am more cautious to recognize that our bodies need to be nurtured and protected. I know that there are times when it is OK to get help from family and coworkers when it is needed. I learned that because I was judgmental toward someone else who had a similar injury, that I seemed to draw this experience into my life. This experience helped me to see first-hand the importance of having greater compassion for others and allowing others to give me the same.

Do you feel that each of your chosen actions /events above has allowed you to experience a greater level of awakening today than when the original event/action occurred? If yes, explain how much time needed to pass until you were able to understand the significance of these events in your life.

Do you feel that *beliefs* and *truths* play a role in either speeding up or slowing down our ability for *Awakening* in our life? Explain why you feel this way.

Homework

Continue to pay attention to any dreams you may have or insights during your day. Keep writing these in your notebook. Then examine them to see if any of these might be related to any of the seven areas of the past events/actions which previously occurred in your life. Look to see if you notice any new information which may help you to understand the reasoning for these past events. Also look to see if it may help you to understand any current situation(s) in your life.

Free Will, and Why It Matters...

I know, as in any field it is important to have a strong grasp of fundamentals before it is possible to move into more advanced topics. It is the same as creating a strong building. First, the concrete foundation must be poured and set. The foundation determines how high and sturdy the rest of the building's structure can be built. This is the same for developing our spiritual awareness. Even those who may feel they have a strong grasp on the essential topics can be well served to revisit studying them occasionally.

There may be a few people who are feeling a bit bewildered at this point, especially anyone who has grown up hearing traditional western religious ideology. Remember that getting pushed out of our *comfort zone* is really a good thing. Feeling uncomfortable hopefully helps us to think about the things we don't normally think about. Then it is even better for us to take action in our life and do something that we might not normally do. Finally, it leads us to creating and transforming our lives into something even greater than before. And this is ultimately why we are here. We are here to create. It is completely up to us. Do we choose to be a conscious creator? Or do we choose to create our life unconsciously? In our boat, do we simply allow the waves to move us in any direction? Perhaps we will go in the direction our parents told us to go, or our friends thought was a good idea, or what our spouse thinks, or our boss or coworker believes is good for us? Or do we actively steer our boat moving through the waves on our own directed course? Do we know how to listen, and trust what we hear to keep us moving on our own chosen course? *This* is what we came here to do.

Many years ago, I facilitated *The Course on Miracles* one evening a week in my clinic. We started with 14 people in the class and completed the course two years later with four people. I recall there was a section of the course which discussed free will. There were a couple of people in the group who debated this topic vehemently for several weeks. The debate was whether the people here have free will, or if everything in life is predestined.

Free will means that each person is free or unencumbered by outside influences to make her/his own choices each day. Otherwise, we may freely choose any thoughts, words, feelings, or actions and create our own life circumstances and destiny.

Predestination means that each person's life circumstances each day have already been predetermined. This means that an outside influence suggested to be Divine in nature creates our daily circumstances, no matter which thoughts, words, feelings, or actions we may choose. A person does not influence any large or small event in one's own life. It is as though a person's life is already mapped out ahead of time.

Many religions throughout the centuries have subscribed either wholly or at least partly to this idea of predestiny. Usually, it is related that this outside influence mostly called

God creates all the past, present, and future events on our planet and in each individual's life.

An example of predestiny is you graduate from high school and apply to go to work at the same factory as your mother. You get hired to go work there. The idea is that a Divine God caused you to do the work needed to graduate from high school. Then the decision you made to send an application to get a job at your mother's factory was really lined up ahead of time by God so the people would hire you. The idea supposes that an outside influence, or God, is responsible for all of these events. Predestination supposes that no matter what your action or decision, the same outcome would occur as your previously determined future.

Now what if we look at these same events in your life as an example of free will? Every day you decided to go to high school. You chose to work hard in your classes, even though a couple of friends wanted you to ditch classes with them. As you were closer to graduation, your guidance counselor showed you could easily enroll in college or technical school. Your mother wanted you to go to college, but you knew that she struggled to pay the bills on her single income and to care for your younger brother and sister. After graduation you decided to apply for a job at your mother's factory even though she wanted you to go off to college. You decided that you wanted to work there for three years until your brother and sister graduate. Then you could help your mother financially to pay bills and save up to go to college later. You were hired. Using the idea of free will, you are moment by moment given choices based upon your own thoughts, words, feelings, and actions. Each day you chose to go to school and worked hard in classes instead of ditching classes with your friends. You were encouraged by your school counselor and mother to continue your education. Instead, you chose to apply to work at your mother's factory and got hired. Although there are several choices of what to do with your paycheck, you decide to help your mother pay household expenses and save to attend college later. Free will supposes that each of your above actions, choices, and decisions were made directly by you and you actively are creating your own destiny moment by moment.

How do we determine which it is? Are our lives pre mapped out for us every step no matter what we do? Or are we truly the ones who always have this free choice within every minute of every day? It is time to become a critical thinker. Unfortunately, too many people these days simply accept whatever someone else says and accepts it as a truth whether it is or not. These types of concepts are what need to be taken through the cascade of questions to determine which of these is a *belief* and which is a *truth*.

One person in our study group years ago really hit on the heart of the matter. He said, "If every day at work and everything we do every day is all going to happen in a certain way no matter what you do. And that means no matter what, it will all turn out the same. Then what's the point? Why would life even matter?"

Those were my thoughts exactly!

Exercise

Review the cascade of questions to assist you in determining A belief versus truth found in the *What is Belief* chapter. On the next page of your notebook, write *predestination* on the left and *free will* on the right side of the page. Write the numbers 1, 2, 3, 4 each on a different line below each of these.

Look at *predestination* and answer each of the four questions in your notebook. Now look at *free will* and sequentially answer each of the four questions in your notebook as well.

Which of the two have you determined is a belief? And which of the two of them have you determined is a truth? Look at all your answers in your notebook. Did you have any difficulties distinguishing truth versus belief with predestination and free will? If so, explain how this seemed difficult for you.

Homework

During the next 24 hours notice the events and circumstances throughout your day, either large or small. Write in your notebook anything that you experience or witness that seems to reinforce and give you confirmation on whether you determined predestination or free will are based in truth. Write specific examples which you feel seem to verify this for you.

Meditation, The Key to All Mastery

After taking a concept through the cascade of questions, what if you have difficulty still discerning truth versus belief? There is one way for us to experience truth firsthand. We may also obtain answers to virtually anything.

Meditation has been practiced since the beginning of time in all the most advanced civilizations. Most every sacred historical text either indirectly or directly refers to meditation. *The Bible* references it in at least 31 different verses, *The Quran* in 27, *The Orthodox Jewish Bible* in 23, and it is found in *The Book of Mormon* in 28 verses as well.

Recently, there have been numerous scientific studies which verify the many benefits *received* through the practice of regular meditation. Most of the studies consistently show that regular meditation practice increases relaxation in the body and tends to normalize the blood pressure. One study shows that meditators typically need less sleep at night than non-meditators. More research has revealed many physical changes created in the brain.

A study by researchers from Yale, Harvard, Massachusetts General Hospital, and the Massachusetts Institute of Technology verified meditation is associated with increased cortical thickness of the brain. Structural changes were found in areas of the brain that are important for *sensory*, *cognitive,* and *emotional* processing. They were most fascinated to find that meditation practice could change anyone's grey matter of the brain. The study participants were typical people with jobs and families, who meditated on average 40 minutes daily. Magnetic resonance imaging (MRI) showed that regular practice of meditation is associated with increased thickness in a portion of the cortical regions related to *sensory, auditory, visual,* and *internal* perception, such as *heart rate* or *breathing.* The researchers also found that regular meditation practice may slow age-related thinning of the frontal cortex.

Present day science is verifying that which has been known since the beginning of time. The practice of meditation is the greatest vehicle for humanity to *receive* all that we are *aware* of that is possible, and all of which we are *unaware* is possible. Meditation is the gateway which every person no matter where one lives, age, social status, religion, financial position, regardless of *anything*, all have equal access.

The regular practice of meditation is the key which allows us to not only develop a physiologically balanced and healthy body, but to access everything. Meditation allows us to find the solution to any issue. It allows us to experience first-hand that we are truly connected to everything. During meditation we witness through our own awareness that which cannot be described in words, and simply know. This is the means to our growth in awareness in every aspect of our being and life. It is here that we encounter the essence of our own reality. We do so by entering the place of stillness, where there is nothing and everything all in one.

Meditation is the one vital practice that every Great Master who has come to our planet first practiced and mastered themselves and then continued to teach others. Since we know that it was a major practice and teaching of the famous Masters such as Jesus, The Christ, and Gautama, The Buddha, then it only makes sense that we should make this our practice too. If we wish to *Awaken* to our own true nature and increase our own awareness, then it is essential we must use this vehicle of meditation in the same way as the Masters.

I know that there are those of you who may find the concept of practicing meditation a little foreign, or even kind of scary. You may be thinking, I don't know anything about that. I don't know where to begin. What if I don't have the time? What if I discover something about myself that I don't want to know? Or worse, why should I even bother as I could *never* be like any of them?

When I first met Sai Maa well over twenty years ago, the notion of practicing meditation was *extremely* unfamiliar to me. Same as with all the other Masters, this was the primary teaching that Sai Maa taught us.

I recall sitting in the group just as confused about this concept as ever. As she was leading us throughout the meditation practice, I kept thinking how I didn't know what I was doing. I wondered if I was doing any of it right and was just sure that I wasn't. My mind was going a hundred miles an hour, into all sorts of ways doubting my own ability to meditate. I saw the others who all appeared to know exactly what to do, following her in the practice. I look back and now realize how crazy it was that I was sitting before a Master who was teaching me directly yet thought there must be some special "technique" that I didn't know. My first full weekend retreat I spent with her distracted by all my own doubts of my own inadequacy.

Sai Maa told us the importance of practicing meditation each day. She explained that we should create our own special space in our home just for meditation. We should have our own chair or seat on the floor exclusively for this purpose. A few years later I understood the importance. It is because as your individual energies become accumulated over time in your special chair or seat, it makes it easier to move to a higher meditative state. When you return and sit in the same chair over and over, eventually you will notice that it takes much less time than before to reach a deeper state. Some of this comes naturally due to more practice, and some is because the energy in your sacred space has ramped up and residually stays in that area. We also could place a small table, called a *puja table* in our space. We may include on it photos of the Masters, ourselves, special crystals, candles or other items to create our own sacred space which also assists to increase the vibrational energies of the whole space. It is important that we place a picture of ourselves along with the Masters, as we too have the same Divinity and shall remember fully soon too.

Attending my second retreat with Sai Maa became the turning point for me. During these earlier years Sai Maa would have a two-hour introduction on Friday evenings giving new guests a chance to meet her. She would usually speak to everyone giving a discourse of some fundamental teachings, then facilitate a guided meditation, and finish with chanting(singing) songs. Same as usual that evening, I started into the meditation taking a breath, and still questioning if I was doing any of it "right."

This time it was different. About halfway into the meditation I noticed that my mind finally seemed to stop thinking all the thoughts. I felt myself drifting and into a place where I lost any sense of my outer surroundings, and I was in a place of silence and peace. Then I saw Sai Maa walk into this room and instruct me as she motioned to the surrounding space that," This was where I wanted to be when

I meditate. This was the place that I should come, and I *was* doing it correctly."

Later that night after the program, I shared this experience with a couple of friends. I am not sure whether they thought I was simply being delusional, but I knew absolutely I was blessed to be in the presence of a Master. It was at that moment I realized that with Mastery; everything is possible.

The weekend program continued throughout all day Saturday and Sunday morning. At this retreat we were sitting on metal folding chairs. It was difficult for me on Saturday to stay focused, as after the first three hours of sitting my back side became really sore. Also, I was distracted because during the meditation Sai Maa was getting onto a man who kept leaving his body. Apparently, he was doing it for fun and seemingly to aggravate Sai Maa. I wondered how in the world someone could *deliberately* do that? I figured that I simply must have been the most ignorant beginner in the whole room.

Sunday arrived, and this time I followed in suit with the others by bringing the fluffiest pillow from my motel room. This seemed to help immensely. One of Sai Maa's assistants reminded us just prior to her arrival, that these would be the last few hours we would get to be with Sai Maa for at least a few months. She suggested that we should open ourselves up as completely as possible, to fully experience this last portion of our time with her.

During meditation I decided to simply open myself completely. I remembered the place of stillness I experienced on Friday night and thought maybe I might be able to go there again. I seemed to move to that place of peace easier this time. Then I just completely opened myself up, and allowed whatever might be there to come. Then it happened. Every aspect of my being simply became beyond any words. I could see myself. I was the most brilliant white effervescent light. At the same time, I could feel the light coursing throughout every aspect of my body. The intensity was so strong, I thought maybe this was what happened to people I had heard rumors of having spontaneously combusted into a grease spot. As a Chiropractor, I equated it to feeling every single nerve fiber throughout my body engorged with light, and electricity like it was on fire. Yet it was more than that. I started feeling every kind of emotion possible to experience, especially all the lower ones, as if they were being wrung out of my system like a sponge. The tears were flowing uncontrollably, and the intensity was such that I thought I might start sobbing hysterically from the emotional release. I opened my eyes just long enough to grab a tissue for my nose. I thought opening my eyes might have stopped it. I closed my eyes, and immediately continued the experience. I witnessed myself as a large, formless being of light. Then I saw two other light beings same as I approaching me. One came very close and the other stayed a little further away. I knew the one closest to me was Sai Maa. We each were the same size and had all the same radiance. I was overwhelmed with the combination of brilliance, emotional release, and ecstasy all at once.

During this time, Sai Maa had noticed me in the back of the room and had motioned for someone seated in front of me to check on me. I felt someone's hand lovingly positioned on my thigh checking in on me. Shortly after, Sai Maa ended the meditation and told everyone to take a break.

I opened my eyes. All the sensations finally stopped, leaving me only in a pool of my own emotional bewilderment. I was still tearful as I heard Sai Maa call upon me saying, 'come hear my beautiful child.' She called me to the front of the room to speak with her. The only thing I could think of immediately after, was that maybe I finally figured out how to meditate. And that it was a heck of a lot more intense than I ever imagined!

I approached her, and she asked me how I was doing. I choked up and told her I had thought my body was going to explode. She nodded her head as I continued to tell her that I saw myself. She said *'yes'* in agreement with me, getting more excited. I told her that I saw her too and someone else, and that we are all the same. She kept saying yes, that I was absolutely correct. Then she was just about to explain something to me. I am sure it would have cleared up all my confusion, and I interrupted her to ask a completely unrelated question. Today I know that it is important to *never* interrupt a Master when they are about to give you an important message.

It took me at least two or three years afterwards to fully understand what had happened to me. Had I been patient and allowed her to explain, I am sure it would have saved me a lot of time. At that time, I had absolutely no frame of reference for this experience. It didn't fit much of anything I had ever been taught in all the traditional religious teachings from my childhood.

Throughout the years I have continued to actively practice meditation daily and have never had this same degree of intensity experience again. I learned through this gateway, called *meditation,* that we are truly all Divine in nature and the same. We each are a brilliant light-being beyond any description available here, and there is no separation. Each and every one of us *is* the Divine Source. I was so blessed to *receive* this understanding and knowledge firsthand. And it is *only* through *personal experience* that we can fully learn that which is true and eternal. This is why it is so important that we each find the time to practice meditation.

It is the Divine doorway which allows us each to experience everything. A Master will never simply give you the esoteric teachings and tell you that you must accept all which she teaches through blind faith. She will say, allow me to *show* you how to discover the truth to everything. It is through your *own personal experiences* that you will ascertain your own wisdom and truth. Everything which is eternal is simply waiting for us. It is always there. Whether we decide to start seeking now or wait another thousand years it will be still there waiting and available.

Sai Maa would tell us over and over the importance of practicing meditation. Once she was telling us, yet again, that we needed to have a daily practice. One woman argued that she simply didn't have enough time. Sai Maa asked her; do you go to the bathroom during the day? She answered," of course." Sai Maa said, "Then you practice meditation while you are sitting in the bathroom." The rest of us found this pretty comical. But she was trying to get across that it was important to simply get started *somewhere*.

During my first year with Sai Maa, I was like the typical Westerner, who really didn't understand the importance of daily meditation. So, I practiced once in a while when I thought about it. That was about once to twice a month. Then during my second year as I began to understand better, I created a small space as she suggested and was able to practice once or twice a week.

One day I was reading a book written by Paramahansa Yogananda, the first Spiritual Master to come to the United States from India during the 1920's. He also taught all of his students meditation and recommended daily practice. However, the light bulb went off for me when he likened meditation to that of learning to play the piano. (It happens I was learning to play the piano at the time.) A person wouldn't expect to be able to learn to play the piano very well if they only practiced once in a while. One could only expect to learn to play well if it is practiced every day. The more time we spend practicing, the better we might become. This is the same as in the practice of meditation. One becomes better at meditation with more practice. I will add on to his analogy that we have the opportunity to remember our own Divinity, and *receive* more when we practice daily, and are able to increase our time.

Immediately after reading this, I was able to truly get it. I decided to meditate every morning and became very disciplined. I found that soon there was a palpable shift in my life. I started to experience everything in my life differently. The obvious occurred, as well as the not so obvious. I became better balanced and peaceful. I noticed that many things which would have disturbed me before no longer did. Or, if there was an upset in my life, I seemed to get through it much easier and faster. Then the important aspect that I noticed was a gradual and continuous increase in *awareness*. Many aspects of my perception of living here started to change.

I found that within only a few months of practicing in the mornings, that I wanted to practice again during my lunch break. It simply became a habit for me, that I would never wish to stop. Once in a great while if I am somewhere that it isn't possible for me to meditate first in the morning, I feel mostly off balance until I eventually can find some time in my day to reconnect. Today I feel my best explanation is that it is like having a battery, which can go for a little while and then needs to be *plugged in* to recharge. When we deliberately plug ourselves in, we can revitalize every aspect of our life.

There are lots of books and teachers of meditation. What I have learned is that there is no *right or wrong* way to meditate. There are countless different methods, and one works just as well as the other. The important thing is to simply get started.

Often someone new to meditation may get started and feel disappointed thinking that nothing is happening. Each person will have a unique experience in meditation. It is just like learning a new instrument, in the beginning it may be helpful to get some lessons to start. Just because you don't notice anything doesn't mean that nothing is happening.

About three years ago I bought my first bamboo plant. It was pretty small, and I didn't really know much about them at all. I bought it during the first day of a weekend I was at a Chiropractic conference. I left the plant in my car during the day while I was in class. It was during the middle of the summer, and it was at least 110 degrees in my car. That night I took it to my room. Then the next day it was in my hot car again. I finally got home with the plant, and within a day it was limp and nearly dead. No matter what I tried, it was simply too far gone. A few weeks later someone gave me a new bamboo plant and explained to me that bamboo needed to *continuously* have a water source, stay mostly at room temperature, and needed some light. Now a couple of years later, I have made sure my plant always has plenty of pure water and is near a windowsill. I have watched it turn spirals and grow up into a strong and vibrant plant at least a foot taller than it was previously.

My bamboo plant reminds me of what happens to us when we regularly consciously connect to our own source during meditation. Similar to the plant, we slowly and gradually start to spiral upward becoming stronger and more radiant. If we simply forget about that source for very long, or do not consciously attempt to connect very often, we are unable to grow and eventually wilt similar to the plant.

Also, if we look at the bamboo plant everyday it is hard to notice that there is much growth at all. But if I had taken a photo of it three years ago and compared it to today, I would notice the plant has actually grown at least a foot during this time. Likewise, the growth in us from day to day after practicing meditation may seem subtle, but after a period of time the changes will be noticeable.

It is impossible for us to ever be completely disconnected from our own divine source. However, when we consistently make the concerted effort to *plug in,* we will grow and experience transformation in our lives.

Although there are probably countless methods for practicing meditation, the easiest approach to get started is practicing with the *breath.* One of my favorites which I switch around and use frequently includes the use of *affirmations,* or what are also called *mantras.* The other completely non-structured end result of practice is simply slipping into *the silence* and getting lost. The latter seems to simply come over time naturally. This most often occurs towards the end of a session. This silence is the place where the thoughts finally cease, and we *experience* our connection. At the very beginning one may not find the silence. This is fine. It is the same as learning anything new, each person progresses at one's own individual rate. Then eventually after some practice, one may notice for just a few seconds that all the thoughts are gone and there is no notice of the body. It might even feel like you have found a blissfully peaceful new space where there seems to be nothing, yet everything. This experience may be different for each person. As you continue your regular practice, eventually a few seconds of silence will grow to a minute, and a minute to a few minutes or more.

When we begin it is important to be somewhere quiet, and as mentioned before, to use the same chair or cushion on the floor each time. It is important to sit comfortably with the spine erect. Initially, we want to focus our attention on our breath. During most breathing meditations, we should use the breath through our nostrils only and not through the mouth. Close your outer eyes and take a deep breath in and *imagine* that above our head there is a large light in which we are connected. Then we *imagine* seeing a tube of light running into the top of our head, and coursing throughout our whole spinal cord through our feet and into the earth. As we take an *in* breath, we imagine that we are drawing that light above us through the tube into our body and down into the ground. Then as we begin to exhale slowly, we imagine each of our breaths are pushing and pulling this light in a circular motion, throughout the body into the ground and above the head. We *imagine* this cord of light which we are attached, as a bright dazzling golden color. Continue to draw a breath slowly and rhythmically *in* seeing the light from the breath coursing onto the cord of light and increasing its intensity. Then slowly release the breath *out* continuing to watch the pattern of light moving throughout the body. Slowly continue this same pattern of breathwork. If you are a beginner, start out for about five minutes. As you become more comfortable with this practice, you will gradually wish to increase the amount of time. At any time, you may choose to stop the rhythmic breathing, it is okay to do so and sit in silence. This most likely will occur naturally with greater practice. At first many people find it difficult to sit in silence for longer than a couple of minutes. This is all completely okay, as with practice it will become easier, and you will notice that you can seem to stay there even longer.

At the beginning, it is not unusual to experience difficulties in keeping the mind from drifting in its thoughts. You will have times that you can't stop thinking about the shopping list in your head, or the next thing you are supposed to be doing that morning. This is all normal, and it is best to simply allow the thoughts to come, and not to attempt to hold them off. As you continue to practice, this will occur less. However, it is important not to worry about this, as even those who have more experience in meditation still occasionally encounter this too. Oftentimes a new meditator will claim that they aren't seeing any of this *supposed* light anywhere. This is when it is important to simply continue to keep open, and simply use your *imagination*. Imagine seeing the light dancing above your head and streaming through your body. Soon enough you will begin to notice the vast benefits, and subtle energies you may have never noticed before.

"Logic will get you from A to B. Imagination will take you everywhere." - Albert Einstein

Exercise

If you are new to meditation, decide on a particular location in your home which is quiet, and you won't be interrupted. Select a chair that you can use exclusively as your own meditation chair. Place it in this location of your home. Ideally this should be in the corner of a secluded room such as your bedroom or another room where you will not be disturbed. You will wish to obtain any cushions or pillows to make your meditation chair comfortable. Although it is not a requirement to have one, you may wish to find a small end table to create your own puja table. You may place pictures of any Spiritual Masters you choose, candles, incense, special crystals, or other meaningful items which you feel will help you remember and connect to your own Divinity. It is important if you do choose to create a puja table that you include a photo of yourself on your table. This is to serve as a reminder that you are Divine, just the same as any of the Masters, and you are to be honored just the same.

Look at your daily schedule. If you currently do not practice meditation during the morning, what time do you normally wake up? If you are new to meditation and currently do not practice daily in the morning, set your alarm to wake up 20 minutes earlier than usual. If you currently practice meditation each day in the morning, go to the next exercise. Make a commitment to do this daily. If you are concerned about losing 20 minutes of sleep, the benefits you will receive will far outweigh the sleep.

Commit to practicing this breathing meditation every day for seven days. If you are new to meditation start out practicing for five minutes. Once this seems easier, then you may gradually wish to increase your time. It is important to sit comfortably with the spine erect. Your feet should be flat on the floor and hands may rest comfortably with open palms up on each of your thighs. Initially, we want to focus our attention on our breath. During this breathing meditation, use the breath through the nostrils only and not through the mouth. Close your outer eyes and take a deep breath in and imagine that above your head there is a large light in which you are connected. Then imagine seeing a tube of light running into the top of your head, and coursing throughout the whole spinal cord towards the bottom of the feet and into the earth. As you take an in breath, imagine that you are drawing that light above through the tube into the body and down into the ground. Then as you begin to exhale slowly, imagine the breath is pushing this light back up from the feet through the body and through the head and above again. Imagine this cord of light which you are attached, as a bright dazzling golden color. Continue to draw a breath slowly and rhythmically in seeing the light from the breath coursing into the cord of light and increasing its intensity. Then slowly release the breath out continuing to watch the pattern of light moving throughout the body. Slowly continue this same pattern of breathwork. Continue focusing upon your breath rhythmically in this way until you feel you wish to stop and simply be silent. Then allow yourself to become silent. This may last only a few seconds at first or perhaps not at all in the beginning. This is okay. The important thing is that there is no right or wrong way to practice this. Every person's experience is unique. Don't worry about thoughts which may come, simply continue to focus upon your breath. Start out practicing this meditation for about 5 minutes. Then gradually you may begin to naturally increase the time as you become more comfortable with the practice.

After you have practiced the breathing meditation for at least five days write down what you have experienced in your notebook. Has the practice each day seemed to get easier for you? Describe any other changes you have noticed since beginning this practice.

Homework

Write in your journal any insights, ideas, or experiences you notice during or after your meditation practice.

Universal Law and Karma

Anytime we wish to create a shift of awareness and move actively into the process of *Awakening*, there are a few foundational concepts we must first embrace. I have found that there are three concepts which in my life have given the framework to help understand, and to put everything into perspective.

The first of the three was introduced to me years ago while I was stationed in the Army in Germany. It was about three years after I had given up my self-appointed task to find the 'one correct Christian religion.' After visiting at least 20 or more different churches throughout a year, I decided there wasn't any *one correct* church or religion and had stopped trying to look for anything. During these three years I had simply given up and was no longer actively studying or pursuing anything religious at all.

Then I was introduced to a wonderful woman twice my age, who would sit and teach two of us for a couple of hours at a time about *reincarnation* and *karma*. I had heard of the words but had never been exposed to anyone who might explain them. I knew these were understood more in the Eastern part of the world, but nothing more than this. She patiently answered all my questions, and eventually recommended that I read a book about Edgar Cayce. I read the book as she advised, and this led me to many more books. I think of her fondly as my first spiritual teacher. Another important thing she taught was the important phrase, *when the student is ready, the teacher will appear.* Our paths crossed in the same part of the world for nearly two years. She set me back onto my path of at least actively pursuing knowledge. Hereafter, instead of thinking I was simply off and not pursuing any religious path, I realized that I was now on a spiritual path and there is a definite difference.

The most difficult concept for me, and I am sure for most other traditionally trained Westerners, was understanding *reincarnation.* I know I had the greatest number of questions surrounding this idea.

Reality is merely an illusion, albeit a very persistent one.

-Albert Einstein

I find it amusing that throughout the years there has been such a division between the eastern side and western side of our planet. Just as geography has separated these two regions, so has the primary thinking of the people within these two areas.

Growing up in the west from a traditional Christian-Judeo belief system fosters in most of us a fairly restricted and sheltered way of looking at life. My background was like this, and even during college I remember for my liberal arts degree our advisors did not recommend such classes as philosophy or religion beyond possibly taking a single New Testament or Old Testament class. I remember one student choosing to major in philosophy being chastised by the rest, telling him nobody would wish to hire him later with that type of degree.

I feel that education then and now in the west tends to compartmentalize everything. We tend to separate our courses of study into specific isolated, and focused areas. I remember having quite a heated discussion on this topic with a friend of mine during my freshman year in college. He was very aggravated that we were required to take general education classes for our degree. He felt that since he was majoring in biology, it made no sense why he needed to take any other courses which were not science related. We argued on this matter several times. He could not see the necessity that he needed any courses outside of science. None of the other classes seemed useful (to him) as he planned to have a future profession in science. The last time I heard, he is currently serving as the department head professor of the biology department in a large university.

There are some aspects of our way of education being so specialized as this which are beneficial, but there are other times it is not. When we have so many people who only know one area or have a single specialty, we each seemingly become our own separate island. This creates a society which has several different fields, each focused upon trying to serve its own interests, and often-times ignoring the rest. This also has a tendency to foster an us vs. them type of mentality.

Everywhere we look today we witness this. Whether we specialize as an engineer, hospital administrator, farmer caring for 3000 acres, computer analyst, artist, maintenance technician, heavy equipment operator, politician, production worker, or librarian, we each tend to know only about our own sector or corner of the world. We tend to isolate our attention and concerns surrounding the well-being of the planet from our separated portion. For example, the hospital administrator is concerned about the upcoming Medicare cuts and rising costs to replace outdated equipment, while the farmer most likely is not. Likewise, the farmer is working to problem solve how to get his corn to produce more in the middle of a drought, and the hospital administrator is mostly unaware of farming issues. The production worker who assembles parts for a large automotive manufacturer may be keenly aware of the changes of specifications in a brake system which has been recently recalled in a vehicle, but hasn't any awareness of the work required by computer analysts to check a software program being updated to perform this year's tax returns.

Because of this way in which we have been so encouraged throughout our years of education in life to focus our energy, time, understanding, and talents into mostly one area, we tend to lose the big picture. We each worry mostly about what is happening in our own world and within our own corner, that we somewhat ignore all of the rest. Day to day we usually keep to ourselves, focusing on our own individual itinerary, or "to do" list. Especially today, it is easy to see that our focus may extend mostly to only immediate family, such as our partner, children, and other family members. During the "daily grind" of life, this is about the extent that the average person concerns oneself with on most days.

It would be ideal if at some point in the typical westerner's education, that someone might stop and ask us some important questions. How does each of these areas (health, manufacturing, environment, computer science, art, education, etc.) affect another? How can they work together? How can we bring these together to better serve humanity as an interwoven team, working towards the greater good of all? Obviously, it is not only in the west that this attitude of separateness has become so inherent. However, it is rare for a person during the years of standard education to search for, and elaborate upon, these greater meanings of life, and how everything we do in our day to day lives may be affecting others.

I know for myself, when I first had been given the two eastern concepts of reincarnation and karma, these gave me a new lens in which to witness the world. I was amazed that so many people outside of the western side of the planet grew up having been taught these philosophical concepts, and these were simply an accepted part of life for many of them. I was also upset that I hadn't taken any eastern philosophy courses in college, which would have introduced me to these views a few years sooner.

If we can truly grasp and understand the meaning of karma and reincarnation, then we are truly on our way to understanding how every living being on this planet is interconnected. This can become our own natural response to moving into a higher overview of life here. Rather than taking the approach of my separate corner and my own needs, we may begin to approach life here as our connected needs and eventually such ideas as *our* greater good. We can then begin to take a greater responsibility for our own actions and their effects on everyone. Instead of thinking day to day, how may I serve myself and my family? This shifts and becomes how may I best serve the needs of us all.

Throughout the years I have come to understand karma to be that which truly is the equalizer. It is really that which makes the playing field for everyone truly level. *Karma* is simply the law of cause and effect. Everything that we think, say, feel, and act upon has a creative energy which we may call the cause. And the degree or quality of the energetic level which is behind the thoughts, words, feelings, and actions are that which determines the eventual outcome, or effect.

This concept is also contained in most of the western Christian Bibles and is stated 36 times in a variety of ways. It states in Galatians 6:7:....*for whatever a man sows, this he shall also reap.* Then 2 Corinthians 9:6 states: *Remember this: whoever sows sparingly will also reap sparingly, and whoever sows generously will also reap generously.* It is apparent this is the same concept as karma, and similarly describes the act of sowing as the same as the cause and reaping is the same as the effect.

A few years ago, this law was a little more difficult to see and visualize in our daily lives, as the effects were slower to be noticed and occurred over a longer period of time. Today because everything is going so much faster, we can see this law manifesting much more quickly in our day-to-day lives. This law may affect us in either smaller ways, or in very large ways depending upon in what way we are creating in our lives using these energetic potentials.

Most of us have experienced a day when we notice generally everything seems to be going wrong. It may start with one simple event, such as arriving at work and finding out you have a mandatory meeting that you must attend and realizing that you are completely unprepared. Then your emotions begin to race, and you maybe become angry at yourself for forgetting and quickly you begin to throw together everything you should have done one or two days earlier. Later that morning, one of your co-workers suddenly makes a couple of sarcastic remarks as though she is upset at you about something. This catches you completely off guard as well. Your day becomes so busy that you don't have enough time to make any preparations for your meeting. You decide to take a shorter lunch, so you have more time to get ready. Just before lunch you are given an insurance form that must be filled out that day for a patient who is coming back to pick it up that afternoon. After you return to work, after lunch you notice that someone has hit your right front bumper on your car. You finally take a long deep breath and think, "What in the world am I doing to bring on all of this?" This is an example of how very quickly our thoughts and feelings about even one single event can draw a whole set of lower energetic situations right to us.

On the other hand, hopefully most of us have had days when we awaken and just feel awake, alert, and happy. Perhaps the evening before we had some good quality time with our loved ones and were able to talk and have some fun. We start our morning smiling thinking about incidents from the previous night. Maybe we will start singing in the shower and smile as we notice that our version of a popular song sounds almost like the original artist's. We go to work that day, and just feel like we are in the flow. Everything we do just feels right. During the day we think about how much we love our work, and all the people we can serve. That same co-worker you had trouble with a couple of weeks ago opens up to you, and both of you can talk out your differences and greatly improve your relationship with each other. Later in the day you receive a couple of compliments. That evening you stop off at the store, which is really busy, and you are able to find a parking spot open close to the front door. During this day our higher feelings and thoughts of joy, and love brought the situations which most closely match that energetic level to us.

This law of karma is constantly working in our lives whether we are aware of it or not. This is much like the law of gravity. This law works in our day-to-day lives and is ever present on this planet and is similar to karma in that it is an unseen energy. Gravity and karma are also alike in that both laws are continuously working whether one believes in them or not.

As a child I remember the superman cartoon being everyone's favorite. Every boy (and some of the girls) wanted to be just like superman. I can remember one very valiant boy getting a superman costume for his birthday. The first day he proudly dawned his costume for all the kids in the neighborhood to see. He ran throughout our yards and the street, seemingly as if his new outfit gave him all the powers of superman. At one moment, he was so convinced of his newly found abilities that he climbed a ladder onto the roof of his garage. We watched him announce one last time, "I am superman, and I can leap the largest buildings and can fly!" His feet clambered quickly and sure across the shingles on the roof of his garage, his right arm flung straight out in a perfect fist fitting for superman himself. As he reached the edge of the roof and took a giant leap, he didn't fly. He fell straight down onto the ground, and fortunately only broke his arm. All his strongest beliefs still could not take away the effects of the law of gravity.

Similar to this, our beliefs no matter what they may be cannot take away the effects of the law of karma. A person may choose to disregard the fact that karma plays a huge role in each one's life and continue to live a life having a point of view of ignorance. Or we can decide to embrace and understand how it is that we are creating our own reality each day in our lives. We must come to a place of understanding, that our lives are not simply a large pool of willy-nilly circumstances which are all random. Instead, we must recognize that everything is not all simply "accidental" occurrences, but we have our own control which allows us to move into a place of empowerment. Only then will we be able to see our lives in a way that puts each of us in the true management of our own destiny as an individual, and as our own interconnectedness to all the world.

Karma, when properly understood, is just the mechanics through which consciousness manifests.

-Deepak Chopra

Exercise

Think about all the various events which have occurred in your life relating to your family, career, spiritual community, friends, health, school or otherwise within the last month. Choose one event or incident which occurred that you can recognize that you thought, spoke, felt, or acted upon, and seemed to trigger one or more other subsequent similar energetic events afterwards. What was the initial event or incident? What other incidents did you notice that day or a within a few days afterwards? Write this down in your notebook.

Did this initial event and the others which followed seem to have similar feelings? Describe your feelings with each of them (Example- love, joy, peace, happiness, upset, anger, pain, frustration, fear, sadness, etc.) Journal this in your notebook as well.

Homework

Pay attention during this week to the small or large events and circumstances in your life relating to family, friends, work, or otherwise. Perhaps something exciting happens during your day. Write in your journal the event and think about any feelings, thoughts, or actions you might have had a couple of hours prior to its occurrence, or even a day or two prior. Write down any connections you notice. Do the same for any challenging experiences during your day. Begin to deliberately see if you can link any of your previous thoughts, words, feelings, or actions to current circumstances in your life.

About Reincarnation

The other major concept that many people on the planet (except in the West) simply accept as true is that of Reincarnation. If we truly wish to understand our highest greatest purpose and comprehend the how and why of the law of Karma, we must be able to acknowledge and truly understand just how Reincarnation works.

Reincarnation defined by the dictionary is: that an individual has a rebirth into another body after death. Those who accept this concept acknowledge that we are eternal beings, rather than thinking a person is born, lives a single life, then after death may or may not have some sort of afterlife on another plane of existence. It is the premise that each person is eternal. It acknowledges that each individual has experienced many previous lifetimes in a variety of differing circumstances. The ultimate purpose of these experiences is to grow in our awareness and are also a vehicle for each of us to potentially "cleanse," or clear away some of this past Karma.

Reincarnation occurs because we decide that we haven't learned enough lessons.

-Sylvia Browne

It never made sense to me that certain Western religions teach that a person comes and lives one life, dies and then is simply finished. I wondered how one could make sense of why one person is born into extreme poverty and dies of starvation before reaching the age of two, and another is born into extreme wealth and receives every advantage and lives a long and lavish life. Then there are those who believe that there is an afterlife; but it consists of a place which is either hell, a place where the person suffers for all of eternity, or heaven, a place where the person lives in perfection and peace for all of eternity. Even as a child this never made any sense to me. And what purpose might this possibly serve, and how could any of this justly be decided? It all seemed to be a flimsy view to me even before I reached a full age of reasoning.

However, if we think of the idea that we have multiple lifetimes, then this makes everything have so much more sense. This allows us to see that the universe is truly fair. Everyone has the same opportunities to evolve, grow and experience as another.

As an example, during one lifetime maybe one lived a life in the Army during a war in which he was in charge of taking care of prisoners of war and treated his prisoners badly. Although he had plenty of rations to adequately feed his prisoners, instead he sold them off keeping the profits for himself. Most of them eventually perish due to a lack of food and living a life of abuse and suffering. During his next lifetime, this person, through the law of Karma, is born into a family with one of her parents being an alcoholic. The

68

father uses all the money from the family to buy alcohol for himself and doesn't care about his wife or children. She lives all her childhood being hungry from a lack of food and essential care. Occasionally, her father abuses her physically. Finally, at the age of 12, based upon a school complaint that she had been absent from school for a few days, the police come to the house to discover the girl has been locked in a room and severely emaciated from near starvation. The girl is placed in a foster care home where she recovers mostly physically yet spends the rest of her life experiencing the leftover emotional scars from her father's abuse. This is an example of how reincarnation and karma work together, and what one might experience from an accumulation of extreme lower vibrational energies during a previous lifetime.

On the other hand, one can experience similar effects during subsequent lifetimes from the accrual of higher vibrational karma. An example of this might be that one has lived a life in which she successfully raised four children, and while living on the Ohio river assisted in being part of the underground railroad. She secretly assisted a group of nine other people dig out and maintain an underground tunnel on her property, which helped slave families get from the Southern Kentucky side of the river to the Northern side of the river in Indiana to obtain their freedom. She risked the well-being of herself and her family for over fifteen years, until the Civil War finally ended. She assisted over 250 different slave families to safely cross the river and gain their freedom. During her next life, she was born into a large and wealthy family in Europe. She went to Oxford University for her education and eventually rose to become crowned the Queen of her country. During this lifetime, she again grows and has the opportunity to touch many lives through her service. Although she still faces challenges during her life as may be expected, she is adored and respected by her whole country and leads a healthy, happy, and very long love-filled life.

These are theoretical examples of the way in which reincarnation and karma become the means which allow fairness and balance of these laws to occur in each person's life. As mentioned, this gives us the ability to see that truly every event, and every circumstance in our life has been created by ourselves, and not by some outside happen-stance luck of the draw.

Dr. Ian Stevenson previously researched and documented over 2500 cases of reincarnation throughout his 40 plus year career as a psychiatrist. His research shows that he has verifiable cases of young children, typically first beginning between the ages of three to five remembering details of their most recent past life. The child may remember all types of details, such as location of the previous home, the previous spouse's name, children, siblings and often may even remember the cause of the previous death. Dr. Stevenson was very meticulous in his method of researching each possible case. He typically would interview the child and obtain as many possible details as attainable. Next, he would search and attempt to find the location and family to verify if the information the child had provided seemed to match. Only after he had diligently confirmed all the specifics of the case, he would arrange for the child to go to the location and meet the family. Typically, the child would astonish everyone present with the ability to recall and identify various family members, names, and incidents only that particular deceased family member might know.

Dr. Stevenson had published several books and articles throughout the years detailing specific cases, and all the usual patterns he had noticed which seemed to be consistent with his verified cases. Some of his later studies included the correlations between the children during their current lifetimes having particular birthmarks. He found that these birthmarks seemed to match the same location of certain health conditions or incidents of trauma which occurred during the previous lifetime.

One case he wrote about in his book, Twenty Cases Suggestive of Reincarnation was called "*Sweet Swarnlata's Story.*" Typical of many of Dr. Stevenson's cases, Swarnlata first began recalling details of her previous lifetime starting at the age of three. She was able to give Dr. Stevenson over 50 specific facts of her previous lifetime. This enabled him to locate the family of the deceased person she remembered, and he was able to subsequently verify all the details she had given him.

Swarnlata was born into a prosperous family in Pradesh in India in 1948. At the age of three while traveling past the city of Katni more than 100 miles from her home, she pointed suddenly and told the driver to turn down a road to "my house." She further suggested that they could get a better cup of tea there than on the road. Soon after this incident, Swarnlata began to relate more details of her life in Katni, which her father began to write down. She told him her name was Biya Pathak, and she had two sons. She continued to give a specific description of the house she lived in, and that her family owned a motor car (a rarity for a family in India during this time, and especially before the 1950's). She related that Biya died of a "pain in her throat," and gave details of the name of the doctor who had treated her. In the spring of 1959, one of Dr. Stephenson's colleagues first learned of Swarnlata's case and informed him of her when she was ten years old. He first met with her father and took his notes from him and was easily able to find the home based upon the detailed description of the girl. He met and interviewed the Pathak family living in the home. They were a wealthy and prominent family, who verified that Biya Pathak had died in 1939 leaving behind a grieving husband, two young sons and many younger brothers. The Pathak family had no idea about Swarnlata's family, nor did Swarnlata's family know anything about the Pathak's, as both families lived over 100 miles away from each other.

Next, during the Summer of 1959 Biya's husband, son, and eldest brother journeyed to the town where Swarnlata was living to test her memory. They did not announce their identities or purpose to others in town but requested nine other people to accompany them to Swarnlata's home where they arrived unannounced. The ten-year-old immediately recognized her brother and called him "Babu," Biya's pet name for him. She then went around the room looking at each man. Some she identified that she knew from town, and others she identified as strangers. When she came to her former husband, Swarnlata lowered her eyes as was customary for Hindu wives to do during that time and called him by name. She also correctly identified her son, named Murli, who was 13 years old when she died. Swarnlata even reminded her former husband of a box containing 1200 rupees. He admitted that only he and his wife had known of this and had kept this fact private from the rest of the family.

A few weeks later Swarnlata's father took her to Katni to visit the home and town where Biya lived and died. She correctly described the décor and layout of the home, and trees in the yard during the time she had lived there in 1939. She correctly identified Biya's room and the room in the house where she died. She correctly identified her other son, several of her brothers, a sister-in-law, cousins, a midwife, a former house servant and even the family cow herder.

The Pathak family were convinced that Swarnlata had been Biya in her previous lifetime. They accepted her warmly, and she continued throughout the years to visit and maintain contact with her former family. Dr. Stevenson continued to remain in communication with Swarnlata for at least another ten years. She lived her life normally, eventually marrying and completing an advanced degree in Botany.

Dr. Stevenson's extensive work and diligence with each of his cases, demonstrates to even the most skeptic that reincarnation is not simply a far-fetched theory. He dedicated most of his life to verifying and proving that this concept truly does exist.

On the other hand, Delores Cannon, a past life regression hypnotherapist, dedicated her life to understanding the how's and why's behind reincarnation. Delores Cannon was a hypnotherapist for over 40 years, and initially, like many Westerners, did not believe in reincarnation. She describes herself during the 1960's as a "conservative and typical happily married woman." Initially, she became trained in hypnotherapy hoping that she might be able to help some people to quit smoking or to lose weight, the typical applications of hypnotherapy. Then one day she had regressed one of her clients back to her childhood during a hypnosis session, and then quite unexpectedly, her client went further before her birth. She reported in great detail her decision to take birth "again," and the lessons she was coming here to learn which she had struggled learning in her previous lifetime. Ms. Cannon was really surprised at this revelation, and soon after began to hear similar accounts from many of her clients during their sessions. She noticed even though her clients didn't know each other, they were relating the same types of descriptions during their hypnotherapy sessions. She noticed that it didn't matter what the person's religious beliefs were, as many described a vivid previous lifetime to her. Each were reporting what aspects were successful during the previous lifetime and which things were still left to learn. They even saw how they died, and most described a resting period afterwards, and how they actively made the decision to take birth again into their present embodiment.

When she first started witnessing her clients experiencing these "past lives," Ms. Cannon began keeping scrupulous recordings and notes from the sessions. She noticed that certain topics came up over and over by different people during their sessions, and she was able to group them into different categories. Ms. Cannon out of "her own curiosity" started researching, and finding as much information as possible on the periods of history and various subjects which her clients were describing. Nevertheless, she found that all the accounts each person had recounted during the session seemed to not only verify various periods of history she had researched, but also seemed to fill in the gaps and elaborate more on areas not described in any of the documented sources. She found that the information seemed to be impeccably consistent from person to person.

Throughout the years Ms. Cannon was honored with several of the highest awards for the advancement in research of psychic phenomenon. By the end of her life, she had written and published at least 16 different books, each categorizing these accounts from her clients into different subjects. She has one which details our common experiences after death and before the next birth. Another book is of those people who detailed a lifetime being with Jesus. One book details people describing previous lives on other planets, and yet another describes how there are three waves of "volunteers" who have come to help the planet earth. Ms. Cannon warned those who read her books, that this new information causes the mind "to bend like a pretzel" into a new shape from contemplating all these incredible realizations about our lives, and the universe in which we are living.

It is apparent that no matter how much one's upbringing has caused a person to become cemented into a belief that each person gets a single shot at life on earth, and we have little responsibility here, all of the evidence from multiple sources shows it is the contrary. Clearly, we can see that our life is infinite, and everything we do creates our own reality and has purpose and meaning. Now it is time for us each to decide whether we wish to continue to take the easy way, avoiding taking responsibility for our own lives and actions, or if we will step up and acknowledge that there is a higher purpose which we each must realize. These concepts have been taught for hundreds, if not thousands of years in many of the Eastern portions of the world. If we truly wish to understand who we are, and how to live our life more fully, enabling us to learn to heal at all levels, we must allow ourselves to embrace these concepts, and to grow and become awakened.

My beloved Sai Maa often during our spiritual retreats will often tell us," I am here for those of you who want to do the work and go fast. I fully respect the ones who choose to go slower, I have no problem if that's what you wish," she gives us a huge smile and snaps her fingers rhythmically into the air, "but you know how I am, I like to do everything fast!"

There always comes a place in our lives where we must make a decision. Do we plan to take the fast track? Or continue to move about the same as always. The fast track always involves us taking action. The slower way always involves us avoiding taking active steps in our life.

The term ignorance is defined from the dictionary as: The state or fact of being ignorant: lack of knowledge, education, or awareness. I feel that there are two types of ignorance. There is the type of ignorance wherein the person truly has a lack of knowledge or awareness as described in a certain area or topic. Then there is another type of ignorance where one truly is aware of a concept or truth and chooses to ignore it. Rather than embracing the concept, it gets pushed to the back burner, thinking if we ignore looking at it completely, maybe this will be easier. However, this merely puts it off until later, and at some time it will have to be faced.

The doorstep to the temple of wisdom is a knowledge of our own ignorance.

-Benjamin Franklin

So, once we are informed, and have been given the framework of certain laws and truths to move forward and take action in our lives, what is our choice? What actions will we take? Or will we not do anything? Whether we assertively take control and move forward, or passively stand by and ignore or resist everything, these are each a decision. These alone determine whether we are propelled forward on the faster journey of *awakening,* or stay rooted in the same slower safe pattern of simply existing and doing the same thing over and over. Those taking the safer and slower route may expect to spend much more time being born again and again recycling here through many more incarnations. But once one finally chooses to awaken, it is even better to reach out and to learn our needed lessons through taking full action.

Exercise

Think about a time during your life in which you went to a place or location for the first time and had a feeling like you had been there before. Describe in your notebook what happened and how you felt there. How did it seem familiar to you? Did you notice any triggered feelings or unusual memories while you were there? What were they? Write these in your notebook.

Think about a time when you first met someone in your past and noticed that it seemed like you knew the person before. Maybe you noticed that you simply clicked and were able to talk with them as though you had known them for a long time. Describe what happened and how you felt during this first interaction. Did you continue to maintain contact with this person? If so, what is the relationship like today? Write this into your notebook.

Have you ever noticed a time that you first met a person and had an immediate strong adverse reaction towards them? Perhaps you simply felt that you didn't like this person, and yet had no recognizable grounds to base this feeling upon. Describe what happened and how you felt. Did you continue to maintain contact with this person? If so, what is the relationship like today? Write this down in your journal.

Have you ever noticed either as a child or adult that you have a particular talent that just came very easily for you? Maybe there is an area that you seemed to need very little instruction, and you were simply able to do easily. It might be drawing, art, writing, reading, building, singing, mechanics, playing a musical instrument, growing plants, or a myriad of other things. What were you able to learn easily? Describe what led you to discover it? Did it simply feel like you already knew how to do the activities, and were simply being reminded? Are these activities still a part of your life? If so, in what way? Write these down in your journal.

Have you ever had a dream during your life which seemed to realistically detail another possible lifetime? What was it? Did it seem very convincing and familiar? Were you able to see any kind of parallel situations which were occurring during your life at that time similar to now? What did you notice? Write these answers in your journal.

Are there certain types of furniture, clothing, cars, homes, music, or other styles that you seem to feel drawn toward which are from a certain era of the past? What are they? Write these into your journal.

Look at each of your answers to these questions. Do any of these give cause for you to see the suggestion of reincarnation? Look at each one of these and describe how you feel this has impacted your life today. Are you able to spot any possible patterns? If so, what do you notice? Write this in your journal.

Homework

Write down any dreams you have during this time. Look to see if you can see any direct or indirect messages which may be related to these exercises. Pay close attention to any flashes of insight you may notice regarding any lessons you may be currently working on in your life. Write them down. Think about how these may be affecting your life right now.

Moving From Fear to Love

I remember growing up there was one of the kids in my neighborhood who always seemed to have many conflicts, arguments, and eventually fights with me. As the only girl growing up in an all-boy neighborhood, this one boy was always stirring up trouble with me and I would never back down from him. Commonly we would chant at each other," Sticks and stones may break my bones, but words will never hurt me!"

During those turbulent years living on my street, I had been taught to say these words and did just that repeatedly. As I continued to grow up and eventually moved away from this harsh conflict, this belief seemed to stay attached to my way of thinking. Even during high school and college I recall discussing this with my friends. We all mostly agreed that it was okay to think anything you want, say anything, and as long as you took no action it was all fine.

Often, we pick up these kinds of notions early in life and may carry them with us for a very long time unless we finally get woke up by the unexpected "bend in the road." I reached my "bend" when I was introduced to my first spiritual teacher while I was stationed in the Army in Heidelberg, Germany.

After she introduced me to the concepts of karma and reincarnation, it was then I first began to realize that not only our actions, but our thoughts and words do really matter. These are what create the reality we are living in our life.

At this stage of my understanding, I first realized there was a distinction in what negative thoughts, words, and actions would create later in my life from the positive thoughts, words, and actions. Several years later I learned that our emotional feelings are also included in this mix and are the main driver behind all of these.

Today I find it better to think differently, instead of positive and negative in relating to thoughts, words, feelings, and actions. Having these as our two categories requires us to make harsh judgments of everything and categorize the world surrounding us as either black or white. I have found this seems to create more separation in our lives. When we look at everything we see and place it into one of these two categories, this causes us to treat them more like things. Unfortunately, this is how the majority of people look at everything in the world most of the time. Another dualist category used by many are right and wrong. This simply leads us into further judgments such as good and bad, and truth vs. false. Taking this approach fosters each person to attempt to categorize each thought, word, feeling, and action of ourselves, and that of those surrounding us into one of these categories.

Some examples of this judgmental duality we see today here in the U.S. are that of the Democratic Party and Republican Party. Many Americans feel one side is right and the other side is wrong, and a few may even think that one is good and the other bad. Each major political issue seems to be split into two sides. Another great example is Religion. Many have tendencies to attempt to categorize once again, into right and wrong, good, and bad thoughts, words, feelings, and actions of specific religious groups.

Of course, we see this emanate throughout the day in our relationships with ourselves, our partner, children, parents, relatives, friends, and co-workers. We are continuously analyzing every aspect of these relationships. It might be, "My Mother and I argue about how I am raising my children, and I feel that she is wrong." Or "My boss keeps showering me with compliments and that makes me feel great." Or lastly, "This is the third time this week I messed up, and this time I ruined the mower when I ran over the rake in our yard. I can't do anything right!" Continually, most of us are evaluating everything in our day-to-day lives just like this.

At least a portion of the population have no idea that in these day-to-day situations, we are continuously creating our own reality in our life. Whether we are experiencing a life filled with conflict, or a life of peace is dependent each day upon the quality of our thoughts, feelings, words, and actions.

When I look back at those tough years as a child, today I am able to see that we had it completely wrong. We were told and believed that all we might say to another, think or feel about others carried no power. We were completely off the mark, as portrayed in the following two contrasting incidents during my childhood.

I had one last blow-out with that same kid just before my family moved out of that neighborhood. I was in the sixth grade, and by then all of us kids knew all the rules, such as we weren't supposed to fight, etc. I was walking home from school late one day (yes, I grew up in the era when most kids didn't ride a bus) after basketball practice. The boy I usually had trouble with was out in the side of his yard with one of his friends as I was walking past on the sidewalk. He lived about four houses down from ours on 34th street. They both stopped passing the football to each other and one hollered," You need to get off of my sidewalk!"

Stubbornly, I stopped and shouted back," This is a public sidewalk, and I have every right to be here!"

He puffed up and demanded," If you don't leave my sidewalk now, I'll just have to *make* you move."

"Oh yeah? I guess you'll just have to *make* me then," I was belligerent and unbending.

He turned to his friend and said," Go ahead and throw rocks at her." He stood behind his friend with a satisfied grin as he watched on as several rocks were hurled at me. Four or five rocks came sailing toward me, none coming too close to his mark. As I witnessed his devious chuckle of pleasure, I felt the swelling of anger within me. I knew I wasn't supposed to throw rocks, but I thought to myself, *maybe it would be okay to just throw one.* I picked up a rock and hesitated just a moment still deliberating, and then pitched it the same as if I were throwing a baseball. (I had a pretty good arm and could throw as hard as all the boys my age and even some older) The one who was throwing at me ducked to the ground just in the nick of time as it sailed across his head. I heard a solid thud as it made contact just below the other boy's right eye. His laugh and giggle stopped abruptly as he touched his face with his hand to find blood, and then started crying and went into his house. As soon as I and the other boy realized he was hurt and bleeding, we knew we were both in big trouble and ran home.

I went into our house and slumped down into a chair in the living room. I knew I was in trouble yet had no idea what to do. I felt bad because I knew better and realized I couldn't undo anything now. A few minutes later there was a pounding on our front door. My Mom answered the door, and shortly thereafter was out on our front lawn with his mother. Years of these kinds of arguments between this other boy and I, which often seemed to lead to fights, now culminated in our two parents in my front yard hashing out everything.

"Your daughter just threw a rock at my son and nearly put his eye out!!"

"There was the time your little angel deliberately pushed her off the neighbor's glacier rock, and we had to have her head stitched!"

"Well, your little darling one time hit him and blackened his eye…"

"And did he tell you that it was because he was strangling a little boy half of his age?!"

"How about the time the neighbor paid your little angel to paint her garage and he threw grapes at it right afterwards and blamed it on her. Did he tell you about that?"

It went on and on seemingly for an eternity. Several years of my facing the neighborhood bully created all of this. I was only brave enough to look out of the corner of the window once and saw both women in a tirade of furious finger pointing, yelling loudly enough that I was sure the neighbors were out on their lawns to see what was happening. When it finally ended, my mom came back into the house slamming our solid oak door so hard that the walls shook. She flew back into the kitchen, and I skulked down into my chair attempting to make myself as small as possible. I was surprised that she didn't say a word to me, and I didn't get into any trouble. Being a witness to all of that probably was torture enough. That was my last fight with any neighborhood kids.

Although this is an example of a juvenile situation, it works the same for any situation. We might start out thinking a certain way, which leads us to use our words. Once we begin to speak our words, these can become emotionally charged with our feelings. Once our feelings become activated with heated emotion, it is easy for these to escalate into actions which may possibly become harmful.

A few months after this my family moved, and I found myself in a completely different neighborhood and environment. I managed to make several new friends in the neighborhood, and the dynamics of my day-to-day life morphed into nearly the opposite of my previous experience. There were kids on our street ranging from ages 6 to 15. There wasn't any fighting amongst us. Those of us who were a little older watched out for the younger ones. We played together, helped each other do outdoor chores and gardening, and if there ever were arguments, they were always short-lived and reconciled nearly immediately.

Then it finally happened that all this harmony was challenged. I was about to enter high school, and we had an exchange student about my age come stay with us for a month in the summer. Delia seemed very charismatic and was able to get along with my friends right away. She was quite a storyteller and captivated the others as she described her typical home life. She enamored others about the lavish-sounding lifestyle of hers with having lots of clothes, and parents giving her everything. She also claimed to have at least two different boyfriends back home. I eventually began to wonder about some of the stories, as some seemed almost too good to be true.

Nevertheless, after about three weeks into her stay, everything started to go a little sour. She began telling my different friends a variety of hurtful things about each of them, which she insisted I had shared with her in confidence. I was oblivious to what she was doing. One by one, each of my friends stopped wanting to see me as she systematically continued to drive a wedge between us. Within a few days nobody on my street wanted to have anything to do with me, and I was completely clueless. She finally returned to her home, and I felt like all my once great friends had abandoned me.

Slowly, one by one each of my friends came to me and asked me directly if anything she had told them was the truth. After openly answering all their questions and explaining that all of it was simply made up by her, they decided mostly as a group that I just couldn't be like she had told them. Within a few short weeks, we became a close-knit group of friends just as we had been before.

Here is another example of a group of young people which demonstrates these principles. Everyone mostly had thoughts, feelings, and words toward each other that came from a place of cooperation, kindness, respect, and love towards each other. So, this created a group of kids who were in harmony with each other, and those surrounding us. Even when one person came from outside our group attempting to highjack this peacefulness through misleading words and actions, the group was able to eventually see through the disruption. They were able to return very quickly back to a place of support for each other again. Whether we are looking at the experiences of children or adults, the dynamics of what is occurring are all the same.

Today, I can look at both of these nearly opposite living situations during my youth and see that these experiences helped me to learn first-hand early in my life about the two types of energy. Obviously, when I lived on 34th Street this demonstrated that if we allow ourselves to be in an environment filled with lower energies such as jealousy, pride, and anger, it is difficult to avoid getting caught into this web with others. The more we are in these lower situations, the more we become this way. But if we are surrounded with others who mostly live from the higher energies such as love, cooperation, and kindness then this is what we reflect toward others and become.

The miracle is being able to have this discernment from these two contrasting experiences and deciding to turn away from those lower energetic situations and people. This allows us to look at life from yet another perspective. If we can start to look at everything in terms of energy, we may begin to see ourselves and the world around us as though we have replaced our glasses with a new set of lenses. As we are able to do this, there becomes less conflict and a greater ability to have peace in our lives.

This newer paradigm is simply that everything is energy. The dictionary defines energy as: a fundamental entity of nature that is transferred between parts of a system in the production of physical change within the system, and usually regarded as the capacity for doing work. Energy is that invisible "stuff" that science at times can measure, but most of the time cannot. It is found in everything, everywhere and is essentially the responsible catalyst for all we can see and that which we cannot. These "newer energies" we are more recently recognizing are those which mostly are the ones science has difficulty measuring. The field of quantum science is witnessing the effects of these but are still at a loss to completely understand them, as they do not follow the typical rules used in the standard scientific method.

Further, if we look at these esoteric energies instead of from the more limited thinking such as good and bad, right, and wrong, positive, and negative and instead use the two categories of high energy and low energy, these seem to fit better and open us up to a whole new realm of possibilities.

When our thoughts, words, feelings, and actions are a higher energy, they carry a higher vibration or frequency. These are those which typically create expansion, openness, and freedom. Those which carry a lower vibration or frequency typically will manifest contraction, a feeling of isolation or restriction in our lives. The higher energies typically are uplifting, and the lower energies generally deflate or depress us.

One of our simple technologies we have had at least one hundred years illustrates this concept easily. If we look at the blades of an oscillating fan while it is turned off, we can see there are four of them- all solid, gray colored, and metal. The blades of this fan are an example of a lower vibration. They are tangible, solid and can be seen. If we turn the switch of the fan on to a high setting, within a few seconds we no longer see the blades of the fan. They can no longer be seen, nor determined whether they are solid, or any color. This demonstrates a higher vibration, or frequency. The blades of the fan are now spinning fast enough that we can't see them, yet they are still there. We have the evidence from the cool breeze they create, yet we cannot see the blades which are too fast. Just as it is possible for the blades of a fan to oscillate at a high enough rate of speed that we don't see them, the same is true for the vast sea of invisible energies swimming all around us. Similarly, most of these energies are unable to be seen with our outer eyes.

During the 1960's Dr. George Goodheart, a Doctor of Chiropractic, was the first to determine that the physical body can be strengthened or weakened by unseen energies. Dr. Goodheart founded and developed his findings into an elaborate technique based upon this simple premise. It is presently called Applied Kinesiology and is today one of several Chiropractic techniques frequently used by a significant portion of the Chiropractic profession. During more recent years, it has been picked up and used somewhat by other health professionals.

When Dr. Goodheart first was developing this technique, many Doctors were initially resistant and even skeptic to the idea that there could be unseen and unmeasurable energies affecting the body. Furthermore, he determined that it was possible to find specific areas in the body which are weakened, then treat these in a certain way which would allow the body to become stronger and function at a higher level.

The basic method of Applied Kinesiology is that the Doctor, or Practitioner first isolates a specific muscle or muscle group in the body to test, usually in the arm. It is then tested using firm pressure by the Doctor. The patient is told to resist this pressure. Once it is determined that it is initially a strong muscle, then this muscle group is used as an indicator muscle. Either the Doctor or the patient can touch other specific areas of the body, and the strength of the same indicator muscle gets tested again. If the muscle stays strong, that indicates the area which was touched of the body is strong. If the previously strong muscle becomes weak instead, this indicates there is a weakness in that related area. Once a particular area of the body has been isolated and found weak, a variety of treatments may be utilized such as specific Chiropractic adjustments, nutrition, and others. After these treatments are administered, the Doctor retests the same previously weakened area. If the treatment(s) which were given strengthen the previously localized weakened area, we will find that the previously weakened indicator muscle test will now test strong again.

Many Doctors throughout the years have built highly successful practices using Applied Kinesiology in their clinics as their major technique to help people heal. Many of their patients will come to them after having had all types of other traditional medical lab testing and treatments with minimal success. Often by using Applied Kinesiology the Doctor may find one or more specific weakened areas, or organ systems of the body which were not indicated during lab testing which may then be treated. These findings in the body are what is called subclinical. This means we can find an underlying weakness in the body much earlier than it will typically show up in traditional lab testing. Once these areas are found and treated holistically, this helps to prevent these imbalances from developing into major health conditions.

Much has been accomplished throughout the years as several Doctors have expanded the use of Applied Kinesiology. Today it is used not only as a tool to help facilitate healing the physical body, but also is used to assist patients improve their emotional well-being.

We had a breakthrough during the late 1990's which shook up and surprised even the Holistic Health Community. Dr. David Hawkins, A Doctor of Medicine specializing in Psychiatry, published his first book of several. This book was a synopsis of his years of clinical study. He constructed an elaborate numerical system using Applied Kinesiology to measure the energetic levels of specific thoughts, words, feelings, and actions of each person.

He tested these over a period of years on well over one thousand people and found that every person reacted consistently the same. He was able to determine that higher energy thoughts, feelings, words, and actions always in every person strengthened them in a tested indicator muscle, and every person was weakened by lower energy thoughts, words, feelings, and actions. Dr. Hawkins found consistently which of these are lower and higher, and more importantly, that every person he tested was either strengthened or weakened by the same ones. His system describes a total of seventeen different energetic levels. Each of them has its own relative position and qualities on the numerical scale.

The first and lowest energetic level on his scale is shame (calibrating on his numeric scale at 20), then the next higher is guilt (30), followed by apathy (50). The next is grief (75), then fear (100) followed by desire (125), next anger (150) and finally pride (175). Each of these energetic levels are shown to weaken a previously strong tested indicator muscle. The first energetic level which maintains the strength of a strong tested indicator muscle, and he considers the lowest of the higher energy levels is courage (which calibrates at 200). The next higher energetic level is neutrality (250), then willingness (310), acceptance (350), then reason (400). The highest energetic levels he determined were love (500), then joy (540), and peace (600) and lastly, the highest possible energetic level he determined is enlightenment (700-1000).

This seemed to be quite a turning point for us. It was the first time that a well-respected Doctor and researcher articulated in such a detailed and consistent manner that everything a person may think, feel, and speak carries a measurable and demonstrable energetic level. These range from the lowest possible state, all the way to the greatest known energetic state. Another component of his research also indicates that people as individuals, people as groups, and even particular actions or events can be calibrated numerically. Once doing so, it can be determined which one of the above seventeen listed energetic levels it most closely matches in its resonance.

During 2001 I attended a large Chiropractic conference in Las Vegas. Dr. Deepak Chopra and Dr. Wayne Dyer both participated as speakers. Both were enthusiastic and elaborated on Dr. Hawkins's new book appropriately named, *Power vs. Force*. They were excited to get the word out, and I shared their enthusiasm after reading his book. There were many of us feeling elated that a whole new door of possibility and understanding had just been flung wide open.

Not only did his work open a completely new area for all Health Professionals to investigate, but this seemed to undeniably show that these energetic levels truly exist. So not only may we correlate that these different energetic levels are connected to the health and well-being of each person, but his research shows these are also related to specific levels of human consciousness.

His work is monumental in allowing us to truly recognize that there is a hierarchy of incremental energetic levels we are continuously creating in our day to day lives. The way in which these energies become manifest is through our thoughts, words, feelings, and actions which either are serving our highest and greatest well-being or are serving to disempower us.

It is important for us to look at all these elaborate distinctions of energetic levels and to make them easier for us to understand. All of the Great Spiritual Masters have always been teaching that there are really only two types of energetic types on this planet which are Love and Fear.

Interestingly, even with Dr. Hawkins's breakdown of his seventeen different levels, it is possible to place each of these into either that which strengthens founded in Love, or that which weakens based in Fear. If we list every possible energy that a human being can experience, it will fall into one of these two categories. So, Enlightenment, Peace, Joy, Love, Reason and Acceptance are all founded in Love. Pride, Anger, Desire, Fear, Grief, Apathy, Guilt and Shame are each rooted in Fear.

Any feelings, words, thoughts, and actions we may experience can easily be placed into one of these two categories. Everything which has a foundation centered in Love will feel uplifting, create expansion, higher growth, and awareness in our life. All which is centered in Fear will feel more contracted, create diminished capacities, and lower awareness in our life.

A few examples which emanate from the position of Love might include stopping to help someone pick up the groceries she just dropped onto the ground. Reading a book to a two-year-old child. Sitting for 30 minutes in meditation and experiencing the stillness. Really listening for a few minutes as a friend tells you she is struggling in her recent divorce and encouraging her that it is okay to love herself and take care of her own needs. Taking a walk in the woods and sending a silent blessing to two deer in the distance, and feeling how grateful you are for the trees, grass, wildflowers, and wonderful fragrance of spring you enjoy.

Likewise, we can determine if our feelings or actions are out of Fear. Examples are telling yourself the recent end of a relationship probably wouldn't have happened if you were a better person. Treating a co-worker poorly because he recently was selected for a promotion you had hoped to receive. Yelling at a child who just ran over your newly planted flowers on her bicycle. Avoiding looking at a homeless couple holding a sign near the road as you drive past thinking, "They should get jobs." Laying on your horn at the driver in front of you who sat through most of a green signal, because you didn't make it through the light.

The differences of these two groups at first may not be the most obvious and may take a bit of discernment to distinguish for some people. The first step is to become aware. Even a few may wonder, why in the world is this so important? Why do we want to be able to place everything we might think, feel, say, or act upon into a certain category? How might this serve us?

The importance is that this understanding is key to enabling us to move ourselves to a greater level of awareness. When we move throughout our life clinging to our old fear- based consciousness, we not only do not, but cannot move into a greater level of awareness. A higher state of awareness not only includes being at an elevated energetic state involving our spiritual levels, but also encompasses all aspects of our physical and mental well-being. If we work to spend most of our time focused on love-centered vibrations, this is a huge key to assist the body to heal at every level.

My Spiritual Teacher, Sai Maa, for years has been teaching these concepts. I recall her instructing us that as we first become aware of our thoughts and feelings and attempt to shift our thinking from fear-based to love- based, that we should try to be easy on ourselves. Maybe as we first begin, we might have 200 thoughts each week based in fear. As we start to become more aware and make changes, maybe the following week it will be reduced to 160 during the week. Possibly the next week it drops to only 120. As we continue to be diligent in our practice, it may gradually drop to as few as 20 or so of these types of thoughts during the week. Sooner or later, these lower energies will lose their grip, and instead mostly the love-rooted energy is what will propel our life forward. This is the foundation to healing. Absolutely no healing may occur without love being present. The greater amount of love we experience day to day directly correlates to the health and well-being of every aspect in one's life.

Sai Maa gives us the analogy that it is similar to us having two plants in our life. One plant represents love and the other fear. Every day we water either one or the other. Each time we think, feel, speak, or take a lower action, we move to the fear plant and give it water. If we continue to do this, obviously our life will become a well-rooted plant of fear. If we spend our day moving over to the love plant and pour water on it throughout our day, then conversely our life will have this elaborate-rooted plant of love. When we quit making trips over to water the fear plant, it will eventually shrivel and die away. Our life would certainly improve in every aspect if its foundation is based upon love. Once again, it is a very simple concept, but not always the easiest to bring about into our life. It requires that we are persistent in our efforts and are patient with ourselves.

During the 1960's The Beatles returned after spending a period of time in India. They reportedly had similar realizations after learning from a Spiritual Master, or Guru. Shortly after returning from this experience, the group was inspired to write several songs placing love as the central theme. All these songs moved very quickly up the charts, and became legendary, including the blockbuster hit, *All You Need is Love*. Some Westerners during this time thought the group had somehow fallen away from reality for a while and had become somewhat brainwashed by this simplistic new concept they seemed to embrace. The reality was that the lyrics in these songs were right on the mark, although maybe a few decades ahead of the typical American thinking.

Exercise

Other than the example below, name at least one duality that you have noticed either in your life or society. Do either you or others tend to take one of the two sides and disagree with the others? In what way? (Ex: Democratic Party and Republican Party. Yes, often people will take one or the other side and disagree with the others. There are a multitude of ways in which one party feels the other is wrong and tends to take opposing positions on many issues. These include health care, the national budget, abortion, gay rights, foreign policy, the war(s), education, and more.) Write this in your journal. Look at the duality you selected above. What do you feel is the best way for people to resolve their differences, and to move to a place of unification in the future?

Do you feel that it is important for us to learn to distinguish in our life when we are demonstrating love-based energies versus fear-based energies? Why is this important? Write it down.

We know that our emotions and feelings directly distinguish whether our state of being is in tune with love-energies or fear-energies. Love-based feelings include love, joy, peace, reason, acceptance, enlightenment, courage, and bliss. Think about all the activities which have occurred in your life during the last 5-7 days. Choose one activity or event that you can distinguish was clearly in alignment with these love-based energies. Describe what happened in your journal. Describe some of the feelings you experienced during this activity and write it down.

Fear-based feelings include fear, pride, anger, desire, shame, grief, apathy, and guilt. Again, think about all the activities which have occurred during the last 5-7 days. Choose one activity or event that you can distinguish was clearly in alignment with these fear-based energies. Describe what happened in your journal. Describe some of the feelings you experienced during this activity and write these down as well.

Look at both situations and discuss in what way you feel each situation affected the rest of your activities throughout the day afterwards. Did you notice an increase or decrease in your productivity? Did you notice greater or lesser communication with other people? Was there an improvement or detriment to your overall creativity or the development of new ideas? Did you feel more focused or less focused? Did you feel that you had a greater level of empowerment in your life or less? Write these in your journal.

Look at all your answers and descriptions above for this exercise. Do you feel that it might be beneficial for you to recognize whether your state of being is aligned with the love-based energies or fear-based energies? Explain how this would better serve you in your journal.

Homework

Start noticing your activities and events throughout your day. Are you able to determine whether you are in a love-based or fear-based state of being? Write these down in your notebook and distinguish whether your feelings and reactions were aligned with love or fear. Look at the activities which you identified as love based. For each of these answer the same questions listed in the exercise at the top of this page. Write in your notebook any new realizations or 'aha' moments you may have experienced as a result of doing this work.

The *Love* Energy

There are four major areas or components we must focus upon developing in our life when we choose to actively pursue *Awakening* in our life. Much like the four legs of a chair, all four are required for a chair to be fully functional. If any one of the legs of a chair are either weaker than the rest or non-existent, then the chair is not useful. Likewise, if we ignore any one or more of these areas, we can expect much less progress or advancement in our Spiritual Journey.

The four essentials are: *Love, Power, Discipline* and *Wisdom*. Each of these are inter-connected with each other and have its own unique dynamics.

First, we will examine *love.* If we only practiced this exclusively, and ignored all the other areas, we would have great transformations in our life. *Love* is of the utmost importance, yet each of these other components are needed as well.

There seems to be three keys to becoming able to fully understand and practice shifting into a *love*-based life. The *first* is that we need to fully understand that there are the two energies that each person every day we spend our day feeding. We are either making trips to water the *love* tree, or the *fear* tree.

Secondly, we must learn to develop what is called *discernment*. This means: "The ability to see and understand people, things, or situations clearly and intelligently." This is also when we can perceive subtle, and sometimes not so subtle differences and distinctions in our daily activities. I feel this is the greatest challenge for us no matter how long we have been practicing. Even when we fully understand these energies, it can be difficult to *discern* whether we are watering the *love* or *fear* tree. When we are in the middle of some sort of conflict or situation, it can be tough to recognize our own feelings. The best way for us to determine this is to ask ourselves if the way in which we are responding allows us to feel comfortable, light, and uplifted, if this is so, then most likely we are on the *love* side. However, if we notice our experience has feelings of heaviness, discomfort, or in any way irritation, then we are most likely watering the tree of *fear.* The greatest portion of the solution comes simply by being able to recognize when we are reacting in a situation out of a feeling of *fear.*

Lastly, in the cases where we determine that we are handling certain circumstances in our life from a place of *fear,* it is best to fully recognize how we are feeling. Often during our lives, we will try to avoid something which is painful, pushing it away in an attempt to ignore that it exists.

This is like a person attempting to walk down a street having a small barking dog constantly nipping at your pant-legs. Try as you might to push it away from you, it keeps coming back and digging its teeth back into the hem of your jeans. You attempt to ignore the scruffy little dog, thinking maybe if you don't look at him, he might eventually wear out and stop. No matter how much you disregard him, he clings and tugs on you consistently and you can't get away from him. The only way you may hope to get this dog to leave you alone, you first must quit ignoring him and acknowledge that he is there. Then you might need to call out to the people in the neighborhood in hopes of finding the owner of the dog. Once the dog's owner comes and can call him away from you, only then will you be able to walk in peace again.

Often this is just what happens to us. There may be an adverse situation in our life which seems to show up on and off throughout our life. We can choose to do one of two different things. We might decide to ignore it, possibly even denying that it exists at all. Or we may instead face it fully and recognize it. Simply by taking this action we might be able to *discern* how this has become a noticeable pattern in our life. Once we have the ability to recognize that it is impacting our life, we can take the next step to reduce or neutralize its effects upon us.

Once again, we must understand how energy works. When we move a lower vibrational energy into a place of higher vibration, it has no choice but to move towards resonating at the level of the higher vibration. Otherwise, energies based in *fear* will dissipate and dissolve when we move them into the higher frequency of *love*.

Dr. David Hawkins determined in his research, for every individual on this planet who has a consciousness level which calibrates at the higher energetic levels, these higher-level energies neutralize those who have lower awareness levels. So, anything less than a 200 calibration on his scale is associated with the lower vibrational frequencies. A calibration level of 200 or greater indicates the higher resonance frequencies. He states in his book *Power vs. Force,* that during the time he wrote this in the 1990's only 15% of the population on the planet are above the critical consciousness level of 200. This means the other 85% are at the lower levels of awareness.

He ascertained that one person at the level of 300(Willingness) counterbalances 90,000 individuals below 200. One person at the level of 400(Reason) counterbalances

400,000 individuals below 200. One person at the level of 500(Love) counterbalances 750,000 individuals below 200. One person at the level of 600(Peace) counterbalances 10,000,000 individuals below 200. One person at the level of 700(Enlightenment) counterbalances 70,000,000 individuals below 200.

Dr. Hawkins states that during this time there were 12 people on the planet who calibrate at the 700 level. He indicates that all the individuals who have attained these higher levels are responsible for helping to maintain the balance of the planet.

His work also reveals that the average individual throughout an entire lifetime will only increase in consciousness by about 5 points. However, he gives hope for us all by affirming," ...it is possible for isolated individuals to make sudden positive jumps, even of hundreds of points. If one can truly escape the egocentric entrainment of sub-200 attractor fields (*fear*-based energies) ...higher levels can certainly be attained..."

So, this certainly indicates if we make the effort, we can make great strides in our awareness. So how can we *escape* from the lower *fear*-based energies and move into a state of *love* vibrations?

There is a whole organization presently dedicated exclusively to the study of the energy related to the heart in the human body. It is called *The Institute of HeartMath* and has been extensively researching every aspect of the relationship between the Heart, Brain, and Human Emotional States since 1991. One of their key findings' states:

The Institute of HeartMath's research has shown that generating sustained positive emotions facilitates a body-wide shift to a specific, scientifically measurable state. This state is termed *Psychophysiological Coherence,* because it is characterized by increased order and harmony in both our psychological (mental and emotional) and physiological (bodily) processes. *Psychophysiological coherence* is [a] state of optimal function. Research shows that when we activate this state, our physiological systems function more efficiently, we experience greater emotional stability, and we also have increased mental clarity and improved cognitive function. Simply put, our body and brain work better, we feel better, and we perform better.

So, they have coined this newer term, "Psychophysiological Coherence." All their research shows that when we live in this higher energetic state that it allows us to experience, "a state of optimal function...our body and brain work better, we feel better, and we perform better." Thus, this equates to a higher degree of health. One of the other key findings these researchers have found is that the heart in the body disseminates an unseen, yet powerful and measurable energetic field surrounding the human body. They have demonstrated that this field projects several feet around the body, and even appears to communicate with each other person's "heart-field" who comes within a close proximity.

This information becomes significant in allowing us to become aware that science is beginning to validate the esoteric teachings which have been taught by all of the Great Masters throughout time. The heart is the powerful energetic center of the body, and this "heart-center" continuously radiates a high vibrational field surrounding the body.

Sai Maa teaches that the heart energetically has two components, or compartments. The first of which is the center of *human love*. This is the energetic love in which many people mistake through life for *love*. In reality, this is of a lower vibration than *love* in its purer form. This *human love* is usually *conditional*.

This is demonstrated when a person sends out the feeling, "I love this (person or thing) because s(he)/it gives me (something) in return. The person with this type of love will send only what one be*lie*ves to be love, thinking that most likely one will get something in return.

One example of this is," I agreed to help my husband to host a Superbowl party this year at our house with all his friends. But little does he know, that since I helped him, I expect him to help me when I plan my family reunion this year." Another might be heard in the divorce court," When I married you, I thought you agreed to stop spending so much money. I can't stay with/love someone who won't listen to me and is such a spendthrift." Or "Hmm, we gave *nearly double* to our favorite charity more than we did last year, and they didn't list our name in the annual report as a major donor." Finally, "I gave our daughter permission to start learning to play soccer with a couple of her friends, but only if she mows the grass and does all of the yard work every Saturday."

Each of the above examples show a situation in which one person is willing to give to another, but with certain strings attached. The first example shows the wife willing to allow her husband to have his friends over for the Superbowl but has the expectation that he must return the "favor" by helping with her family reunion. The next example as a marriage is ending, there was an apparent earlier promise from one spouse to change the spending habits. Apparently after some time the spouse realized that this wouldn't change, and this was unacceptable behavior to endure in a relationship. This exemplifies a conditional marriage. The third example shows a couple giving to a certain charity thinking that they would receive some type of acknowledgement in return. This action reflects how these people are giving to a cause but wish to be publicly acknowledged for their generosity. The last example shows a parent allowing her daughter to go learn and play a new sport, but only if she works most of her Saturday performing yard work. Again, this is an example of giving a loving action to another with certain conditions attached.

The second compartment of the heart houses *divine love.* This is the energetic love which carries the highest vibration. This type of love is *unconditional.* Divine love is demonstrated *when the person loves someone or something, simply for the sake of loving.* One does not expect to receive anything in return, and the love is ever-present regardless of the situation or actions involved.

One example of this is, "I noticed my wife was up past midnight last night studying for her exams, so I made her breakfast thinking she could sleep a little later." Another might be," I saw someone homeless curled up on a park bench and he looked cold. I went back to my car and walked back to give him my emergency blanket, and I also gave my change I normally keep for toll roads." Another is, "I go up to visit my mother in the nursing home every night after I get home from work. She has been there now for at least two years and doesn't recognize us anymore. I go anyway so she can tell others she has a visitor every day, and somehow, I know she realizes that she is loved." Also, pay attention to your pet dog or cat. Every day they show us affection. It matters not the day; your pet will come running to greet you at the door. They are full of wagging tail excitement, or purring happiness as your ankles are rubbed up by your feline. Your pets always give you the warmest and most loving greeting no matter if you or they had a lousy day. I am convinced their major purpose here is to teach us through bathing us with *unconditional love.*

The first example shows a genuine act out of concern which comes from the higher levels of love. The spouse thoughtfully cooks breakfast to help her have more time to sleep. There isn't anything expected in return, simply a wish to help, fueled by love and concern. The second example illustrates a high level of generosity without any expected return. Assisting a person who appears to be homeless and without enough essential clothing or blankets to stay warm is an act of pure compassion and love for another person. The third example displays the same type of higher love again simply for the sake of loving. Going every day to see your mother in the nursing home is purely unconditional love at its best. The last example of our beloved pets are the greatest example for us to learn to imitate. If we can embody the level of love and devotion our furry best friends harbor for us, we would certainly evolve beyond the need for any further studies or practice. Unfortunately, most of us have quite a way to go yet, but we can still watch and learn much from them.

Unconditional love really exists in each of us. It is part of our deep inner being. It is not so much an active emotion, as a state of being. It's not 'I love you' for this reason or that reason, not 'I love you if you love me.' It's love for no reason, love for no object.

-Ram Dass

Once again, *human love always* has an outright or underlying expectation, and *divine love never* has any expectations. An attribute about the heart-center is that this higher-level *divine love* radiates from here and is ever-present. It is *divine love* only, which will transform and neutralize any lower frequency energies(fear-based).

Exercise

Think about each different area of your life including family, spouse/partner, friends, spiritual, career, education, health, or any other area. Focus upon the one area which you have noticed the greatest number of difficulties for you during the last month. This most likely will involve your relationship with another person in one of these. Identify the #1 relationship that you most notice your tendency to go water the fear-tree the most frequently. Describe what incidents/events happened. Write this in your notebook.

Have similar incidents happened previously? If so, briefly describe these. What is the length of time ago when you first noticed this difficulty first began? Write these down.

Describe some of the feelings you can identify during this most recent difficult incident. During and immediately after the incident were there certain areas of your body that you could feel any discomfort? If so, what did you notice and where?

Use your discernment and look for any potential patterns that you may identify looking at the interactions during the history of this difficulty. Describe any that you may see in your notebook.

Think back to this incident. Did you realize at the time that you were watering the fear-plant?

If not, how long did it take you to first discern this after this incident? Give an example that you have experienced in one of your own relationships that demonstrates the concept of divine love. Describe what happened.

Describe how the definition of divine love applies to this specific occurrence.

Give an example that you have experienced in one of your own relationships that demonstrates the concept of human love. Describe what happened.

Describe how the definition of human love applies to this specific occurrence.

Use your discernment to now examine your #1 difficult relationship you identified in the previous exercise. Look at everything which occurred in this most recent incident. Are you able to discern whether either you or the other person(s) involved were demonstrating either human love or divine love towards the other person(s). If so, which one? Explain how the action meets the definition described above.

Homework

At the end of each day for the next few days take a few minutes before bedtime to review all that occurred during the day. Write in your journal any events in which you noticed that you were watering the tree of *fear*. Describe your feelings during any of the events. Similarly, notice everything you did during the day in which you were experiencing *love*-based events. Describe these in your journal. After identifying any *fear* events, think about what you might do differently next time to shift the situation to a higher more loving event. Write any of these ideas in your journal.

AFTERWORD

As I finish this, I can see distinctly how this book parallels the recommendations I have given my patients in my clinic throughout the years. It is just like when I would give one of my new patients a new diet which lists the healthy foods s(he) needs to consume regularly, and the list of ones which are to be avoided and eliminated. Oftentimes, I see them look at the list like a deer caught in headlights and are quiet for a few moments. They break their silence usually with something like, "But I *love* wheat bread, and eat it with nearly every meal." I smile and tell them to relax, as they don't have to change it *all* overnight. I assure them that I realize that they have been in the habit of eating whatever food choices they have made for years, and simply didn't really know. However, now that they are educated and *know* how to stop buying unhealthy foods, they may start focusing upon buying the heathier selections. The foods that need to be eliminated; they now know to stop buying. Rather than attempting to do everything all at once, I suggest that each week they should *take action* to change only one or two things at a time. Gradually, there is a shift towards eating healthier foods most of the time. Although I have some patients who would simply take all my recommendations at once, it is easier for them take the more gradual approach. There is usually a greater level of success when we make gradual changes, than large drastic ones all at once. The important thing is to take one step, then another, and keep moving forward. Eventually, over a period these healthy dietary changes will allow for the gradual shift of increased health.

One of the greatest discoveries a man makes, one of his great surprises, is to find he can do what he was afraid he couldn't do.

-Henry Ford

One time I recall; I had a patient who called my office who I hadn't seen in well over a year. I recalled that this man, in his sixties, had multiple conditions, including anxiety and depression, diabetes, irritable bowel problems, multiple joint pains, and was obese. When he first came to me his health was spiraling out of control; and like many of my other patients had already been through all the traditional medical care. My treatment recommendations for him included my typical methods of Chiropractic, enzyme therapy, nutritional supplementation, affirmation exercises, and special dietary changes. I recall that this patient was enthusiastic, and wanted to receive *every* treatment that I offered in my clinic, so he even chose to receive a couple of energetic healing sessions as well.

He spoke with me on the phone and said that he wanted to thank me for all the care he had received. He said that he did continue to completely change his diet, and now he has lost over 100 pounds. Not only this, but is no longer diabetic, and is completely off all his old medications. He said that he just took it one step at a time, like I suggested, and now he feels healthier than he could ever remember during his life.

This is *exactly* how slow and steady *action* can create transformative changes in our lives. It works the same way regardless of what it is that we are working to improve in our lives. It is the same if we are working to improve our spiritual growth.

I encourage you during the first week to take *one action step* forward. Then next week take *another step* forward, and so forth. If some of it feels a little uncomfortable, that is great, as this is when we have the highest level of growth. Within a short time, you will begin to see the transformations occurring in your life.

We can easily forgive a child who is afraid of the dark; the real tragedy of life is when men are afraid of the light.

-Plato

As I finally finish this book, it is important for me to share with all of you, the readers, that I am travelling on my own spiritual journey, the same as everyone. Every day I am learning and growing, and within this book I have simply shown you that which I have come to know in my own life. Many of the concepts I learned through my own inquiry, experience, and the teaching and guidance of a living Spiritual Master. The rest of the information simply *came through,* and I was Divinely guided and given much information to share with all of you. I realize that this *guidance* was just as much for me as for everyone else. So, realize that much of this material is new for me to consider and learn as well.

I'm not a teacher: only a fellow traveler of whom you asked the way. I pointed ahead - ahead of myself as well as you.

— George Bernard Shaw

REFERENCES

HTTP://WWW.UCMP.BERKELEY.EDU/GEOLOGY/TECMECH.H
TML

The Center for the Study of Global Christianity (CSGC) at
Gordon-Conwell Theological Seminary in South Hamilton,
Mass. CSGC researchers generated their estimates based in
large part on figures provided by Christian denominations
and organizations around the world. CSGC has obtained
denominational membership information from about 41,000
organizations worldwide.

Cannon, Delores. *The Convoluted Universe: Book IV.* Ozark
Mountain Publishing, 2012.

Stevenson, Ian. *20 Twenty Cases Suggestive of
Reincarnation.* The University of Virginia Press, 1974.

Hawkins, David R. Power vs. Force: The Hidden
Determinants of Human Behavior. Veritas Publishing, 1998.

Walther, David S. *Applied Kinesiology Synopsis.* Triad of
health publishing, 1988.

http://en.wikipedia.org/wiki/The_Beatles_in_India

http://www.heartmath.org/research/science-of-the-
heart/entrainment-coherence-autonomic-
balance.html?submenuheader=3

About The Author

Dr. Jane E. Rackley is a Chiropractic Physician, who was active in private practice for over 24 years. She offered many cutting-edge treatments for her patients throughout the years including Chiropractic, Clinical Nutrition, and Bio-Energetic Healing. As a Healer, she is dedicated to bringing the greatest level of health and well-being into as many lives as possible.

Currently, she has dedicated herself to reaching even more people through her writing. Her mission is to teach others how *every* person can tap into her/his own Divinity and Master the ability to heal themselves. This is her third book which teaches step-by-step how to transform one's life from being ordinary to extraordinary.

For over 23 years, she has been graced with the direct teachings of a living Spiritual Master in her life, H.H. Sai Maa Lakshmi Devi. She has been on her active spiritual journey since the age of eight, and gladly shares all the teachings she has learned to others through her books and classes.

Her previous books include *Love Yourself and Be Healed: Awakening,* and *Twenty Weeks To Transformation: Workbook To Accompany Love Yourself and Be Healed.*

For upcoming new releases check her website at: www.DrJaneRackley.com